April 2009

Harambee!
Stories and Recipes
from the
African Family Circle

Grace Kuto

To San Juan Island library,
Thank you for hosting my
book signing and cooking
class today. Wishing all who read
this best.
Grace Kuto

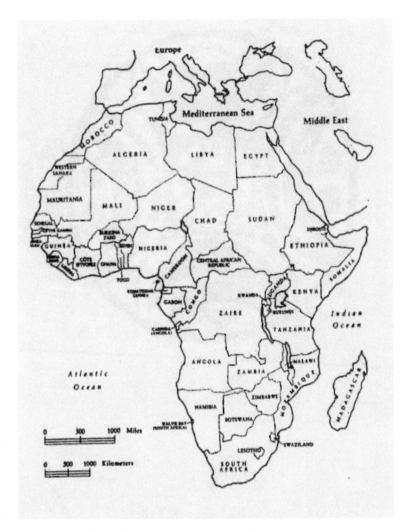

Please note: The names of some of the countries in Africa have changed since this map was published in the original book.

Harambee!
Stories and Recipes
from the
African Family Circle

Grace Kuto

BestSeller Books, Inc.
Wilsonville, Oregon

Let us take care of the children
For they have a long way to go.
Let us take care of the elders
For they have come a long way.
Let us take care of those in between
For they are doing the work.

Traditional African Prayer
author unknown

Top: Grace Kuto with Chwele Clinic staff
Bottom: Gail Winterman, RN with Chwele Clinic staff

Dedication

Harambee Centre is Born www.harambeecentre.org

Harambee Centre, a Portland, Oregon-based non-profit organization was established in August 2001. Our mission is to connect the people of the Pacific Northwest with the people and cultures of Africa through education, cultural exchange and African development programs.

Jackie Goldrick and I discovered our mutual interest about African issues after she had spent about six years in Ghana and Kenya during the 1990s . With the able leadership as Founding Chair of the Board, Jennifer Froistad, *Harambee* Centre was well rooted in its established mission and goals. Our second board chair, Matt Essieh, led us through a tremendous continued growth of projects in four different countries — Ghana, Kenya, Tanzania, Uganda. This growth includes sister-school projects at Southridge High School led by Jeremiah Hubbard with Matale Senior Secondary School in Uganda and West Linn High School led by David Frik with Namwela Secondary School in Kenya. Gerry Uba, Ph.d is our present board chair endeavoring to take us to the next level of capacity development.

The seed of Harambee Centre came out of Chwele community work while the nurturing hands were organizations such as the World Affairs Council of Oregon and Multicultural Resource Centre through education program partnerships. Today we partner with them in bringing African education to K-12 schools through the "Teach

Africa" program. We also have our own resource curriculum for K-middle school called "Africa is Not A Country." I wish to thank the Harambee Centre board members for their diligent efforts of representing Africa in this region with positive and educational programs. Jackie and I are eternally grateful to all the supporters of the work and the African people we represent. Without your support, *Harambee* Centre would not be able to make the difference it makes today in the Pacific Northwest region and in Africa.

— Grace Kuto

Acknowledgements

First and foremost, I want to thank my husband, Paul for his undying support for my writing and his partnership in community outreach. I thank my daughters, nieces, nephews, sons-in-law for making me feel appreciated everyday. I thank my grand daughter, Malaika (Angel) Grace for keeping me laughing with her vivacious smile. I also thank my sister, Elizabeth Bwayo for her inspirational courage. It is her healing that slowly brought back the sun in my heart again for writing.

The encouragement from friends and colleagues, Maryanne Fry, Karen Ettinger, Nana Nash, Thomas Lwebuga, Athina Stillinger, and Dean Jack W. Clinton of OHSU School of Dentistry was especially invaluable in cheering me on to write again.

There are a few other people outside my family to whom I wish to express my gratitude for their enormous contributions to this publication:

- Essieh Family Foundation
- Mark Mathabane for writing the forward for this publication
- Amy Mfuni for the art illustrations for the recipes
- Brian Geraths for the cover photography. Website at www.yourprints.com
- Ursula Bacon for her incredible editing skills.
- Sheryl Mehary for her mastery and text design skills.

Thank you to organizations who contributed to the clinic fundraising through African dinners:
- Oregon Health and Science University
- World Affairs Council of Oregon
- Women of Vision
- Portland Red Cross
- Multnomah Presbyterian Church
- Reflections Bookstore
- Mercy Corps
- Medical Teams, International
- American Friends Service Committee (AFSC)
- Good Samaritan Ministries
- Lewis and Clark College
- Northwest Yearly Meeting of Friends
- Oregon Returning Peace Corps
- Tigard Community Friends Church
- Juneau Friends Meeting
- World Affairs Counsel of Alaska
- Dick and Ellyn Anderson family
- Tom and Marilyn Fink Family
- John and Jane Emrick family
- Peter and Jill McDonald family
- Bill and Laurie Essig family
- Matt and Ella Essieh family
- Chuck and Nancy Marshall family
- Professor Dennis and Janet Hagen family

I owe my thanks to so many others who I am not able to mention here due to lack of space.
Asante Sana!
Grace Kuto

Foreword

Harambee is more than a cookbook redolent with
delicious African recipes. It's an enthralling account of the
essence of Kenyan culture and history passionately and
poignantly told in song, poetry and prose by one of her
loveliest daughters. Grace Kuto is one of the most deeply
caring people I have ever met. She possesses in the fullest
measure what Africans call *Ubuntu* — the quality of being
human. In *Harambee* Grace, who grew up an orphan in
Kenya and has never forgotten her roots and the many
persons who have helped her along the way, invites all
those who care about the state and future of our common
humanity to harness this powerful spirit of *Ubuntu*. She
couldn't be more right and timely. Only *Ubuntu* can
nurture our souls, strengthen our families, heal our
communities, and create a better world for all.

The spirit of *Ubuntu* — whose core is kindness,
compassion, empathy, forgiveness, togetherness and love
— has led Grace to do extraordinary things. In a career
spanning decades and two continents, she has empowered
and sustained the hope of the poor, the powerless and the
oppressed. She has spearheaded efforts to educate our
children about Africa. And last but not least, she has chal-
lenged communities to celebrate diversity and multicultur-
alism as the lifeblood of progressive societies.

The pages of *Harambee*, though providing us with
a cornucopia of delectable and healthy African meals,

challenge all of us to pull together if we are to become better persons and find lasting solutions to urgent problems of how to best educate our children for a global future, provide health care for all, empower marginalized women, preserve endangered cultures, achieve lasting peace, and save the planet. Among the many worthy projects supported by the indefatigable Grace through proceeds from the sale of *Harambee* are a clinic and schools in the Kenyan community of Chwele. So, dear reader, enjoy these mouthwatering recipes, learn a little Swahili, celebrate African culture and, most important, support a dear friend as she strives with joy and love to change the world, one life at a time.

Mark Mathabane
Author of *Kaffir Boy*
Portland, Oregon

Table of Contents

Introduction

Harambee! (pronounced har-ahm-bay) in Swahili Kenya's national language means "let's pull together for the good of global community."

The *Harambee! Stories and Recipes from the African Family Circle* was revised in the spirit of *harambee* to raise funds to improve Chwele Community Development. The first edition of this book fully funded the cost ($50,000) of the Chwele Heath Clinic in my village in western Kenya which now serves an area of nearly 58,000 people.

Traditional African families gather in a circle at meal time and eat together. The circle exemplifies the spirit of sharing and togetherness.

In this edition I have revised some recipes which I originally collected from family members and friends with their permission. I developed some of them by accident, others were born from curiosity. This curiosity never ends, therefore there are some new recipes as well. I have shared these delicious dishes with thousands of family, friends and supporters for nearly 30 years.

I now want to bring these easy and delicious recipes to people beyond the borders of Portland and Kenya. In Africa, the assembling and sharing of food highlights the spirit of celebration and the daily bonding of family and the community. The recipes offer a look at the basics of the African cultural eating habits and values. Traditional African cooking is most adventurous, yet least known in the international cooking arena.

The African continent is vast and is the home for many different people, and it is difficult to characterize some "Africa dishes" as "typically African." The more contemporary East African cooking is influenced by East Asian and European tastes because of the political history these cultures have shared with this particular African region.

This edition covers the traditional and urban cooking of East Africa. In African urban areas herbs and spices are more commonly used. In rural areas, traditional habits of cooking and eating have almost remained unchanged by outside influences. The traditional African customs encompass not just the satisfaction of hunger but are strong means for enhancing family and community ties.

People eating together in the African community is one of the most meaningful aspects of the culture. One rarely eats alone. Food is also used as an expression of celebration at weddings, babies' birthdays or naming ceremonies, community *harambee* gatherings, family reunions, funerals, welcoming guests and so on. A first-time guest is always acknowledged with a feast of a meal. In times of scarcity, not much may be available to share, but the little still must be divided among those in the circle. Western observers are often amazed at the mountains of food which are prepared for typical African weddings. The leftovers are happily shared and bags of food leave the party along with the happy guests.

This book also addresses how traditional African food and lifestyles affect the health of the people. Eaten in right amounts and combinations, the East African diet is ideal for maintaining good health. An average rural African family eats more plant foods than animal foods simply because they are readily available. Meat is not eaten more than two or three times a week — especially in rural areas. Studies point to the long-term health effects the East African diet and the lifestyle have on its people.

A study conducted by cardiologist, M. John Murray, of the University of Minnesota, looks at the specific components of the Masai diet and how it is affected by their lifestyle.

Another recent study conducted by Kenyan medical experts disclosed that incidences of hypertension among the Masai and Samburu tribes are almost non-existent. It proves that those ethnic groups who have maintained traditional lifestyles and diets have managed to escape the dilemma of food and industry-related diseases such as heart attacks, strokes, diabetes, certain cancers and other serious health problems. This book emphasizes the importance of a well balanced diet, rich in nutritional values. Basic nutrition facts are discussed so that the reader has a basic understanding of food and the chemical interactions which take place in the human body.

In Africa, food and hospitality are synonymous with the African woman. A section of this book is dedicated to her contribution to food productivity in her homeland.

I wrote the poem "The Heart of Africa" in memory of my mother, and for all the African women whose strength holds the cultural fabric of their society together.

I have dedicated the poem "The Hungry Child of Africa," to the voiceless children of my homeland. *Harambee* Centre in Portland, Oregon, USA joins the world once every year in the month of June to commemorate the *Day of the African Child* to bring attention to the plight of African children in the world.

Jackie Goldrick with Grace Kuto at first Harambee Centre Fundraiser — 2001

Mini Facts On Kenya

Official name:	Republic of Kenya
Location:	East Africa (see map of Africa).
Area:	224,960 square miles (580,367 square kilometers).
Population:	31 million (2007 census).
Ethnic groups:	40 or more ethnic groups using different languages or dialects. The main ones are: African; Kikuyu 21%, Luhya 14%, Luo 13%, Kalenjin 11%, Kamba 11%, Kisii 6%, Meru 5%. Non-African; Asian, European, Arab combined 1%.
Religions:	Indigenous beliefs 24%, Protestant 40%, Roman Catholics 30%, Muslim 6%.

Languages:	Swahili (national language), English and many ethnic local languages.
Greeting:	Strong firm handshake and eye contact whether male of female.
Education	First four years of primary school are free; eight years primary, four years high school and four years college or university.
Work force:	Total wage earners 1.4 million: public sector 48%, industry and commerce 21%, agriculture 21%.
Colonial History:	Kenya's written history dates back to 1,000 BC. Kenya's proximity to the Arabian Peninsula invited colonization. Arab and Persian settlers were the first in the area about the eighth century. By then the Bantu and Nilostic peoples had already moved into the area. The Kiswahili language, a mixture of Arabic, English and other languages became the trading language. In 1498, Portuguese arrived and took over from the Arabs at the coast. About 1600, the Imam of Oman reigned until the British laid claim to the whole of East Africa and declared the land mass a protectorate in 1895. Kenya officially became a British colony in 1920. From October 1952 to December 1959, Kenya was under a state of emergency which arose from *Mau Mau (Muzungu Aende Ulaya, Muafrica Apate Uhuru)* revolution against the British colonial rule. During the colonial time, there was segregation

in Kenya just like it was in the United States and South Africa. The first direct elections of Africans to the Legislature Council took place in 1957. Kenya became independent in 1963 and joined the Commonwealth the following year. Jomo Kenyatta, a member of the Kikuyu tribe and head of the Kenya African National Union (KANU) became Kenya's first president. When President Kenyatta died in August 1978, Vice President Daniel Arap Moi became the interim president and in October 1978 was elected the second president of Kenya. In early 2008, a Grand Coalition Government was formed under President Mwai Kibaki and Prime Minister Raila Odinga after several months of severe unrest following questionable election results in December 2007.

Main Sources
of Foreign
Exchange: Coffee, Tea, and pyrethrum exports, tourism and petroleum products.

Monetary Unit: Kenyan shilling.

Kenya Embassy: Address: Embassy of Kenya, 2249 R. Street N.W., Washington, DC 2008 — Telephone: 202-387-6101

Kenya Consulate: Telephone: 310-274-6635

Top: Lutomia Kuto working with children on clinic grounds
Bottom: Joella Werlin and Karmin Tomlinson planting trees
on clinic grounds

The Climate of Kenya

The Climate of Kenya: Its Effect on the Culture was written by Jill McDonald, born and raised in Kenya, resident of Wilsonville, Oregon.

It has been said that Kenya has the best climate in the world — and for part of the country this could certainly be true.

Climate, anywhere in the world, influences the types of food people eat, their occupations, modes of transport, their homes, dress and all other facets of life. In fact, weather influences their culture.

In Kenya, because the land varies in altitude from sea level to heights over 17,000 feet, there are areas of desert, tropical forest, dry grassland, alpine meadows, equatorial lowlands, and rich farmland. Each of these regions calls for its inhabitants to make adaptations in lifestyle and so encourages cultural difference between the various tribes. The vast majority of Kenyans live at altitudes of 3,000 to 6,000 feet above sea level.

As a result of Kenya spanning the equator, the country experiences no real winter. Only the wetter periods of the monsoon convey the feeling of having seasons. Regions less affected by rains are the vast deserts or semi-deserts in the north, east and south of the country.

Due to being located in the proximity of the Equator, every day of the year has the same amount of daylight — there is no switch from "Daylight Saving Time" to Standard Time. There is no sunset at five o'clock one day and at nine o'clock another day. A constant twelve hours of night and twelve hours of day is the rule. The sun rises at around 6:30 a.m. and sets around 6:30 p.m. every day of the year.

In the highland regions of Kenya there is sufficient rainfall, as well as excellent soil. Food staples such as corn, rice, potatoes, vegetables and fruits can be grown. The natives have a balanced diet. In the lower more arid areas this is not the case. Many tribes rely more on the meat products from their cattle and goats — no crops are grown there. Along the coastal strip, where the climate is more tropical, fish and coconuts feature prominently in the diet.

Even the dress of Kenyans is influenced by the climate. Throughout most of the country the people like to wear strong bright colors: reds, yellows, blues, greens, pinks and oranges. These hues match the bright sunshine. Some exceptions to this are the Masai, Turkana and Samburu people who live a nomadic life. The wander over the hot, dusty plains with their herds of cattle and goats. They have largely retained their preference for using earthy tones in their garments — especially the reddish brown blankets in which they wrap themselves. Another exception is the women from the northeastern and eastern regions who, because of their Moslem faith wear black robes. The men of the coastal region are often seen in white clothing, which reflects the extreme heat.

The types of homes in which Kenyans live are affected by climate and location. As a result of the arid climate which dictates a nomadic lifestyle, the Masai, Turkana, Samburu and other pastoral tribes had to be able to literally "pick up stick" and move their houses frequently in order to gain access to fresh grazing land for their herds. They have largely built easily moveable homes which can quickly be reassembled. Traditionally, the homes of farming peoples from the higher, fertile, more temperate regions have been constructed for permanence from the products of the forests and grasslands that surround them. In this region, the nights can be quite cold so the need for warmth and a good chimney hole is important. The rondavaal made of mud and wattle, was the traditional home of Kikuyu and other tribes. More recently these have been replaced with larger, even longer-lasting, wooden and stone structures. The residents of the hot coastal lowlands need their shelter more from the heat than from the cold. They have cut the poles for their homes from the nearby mangrove swamps and roofed them with palm fronds.

People from the agricultural highland, which has a climate that allows for the constant renewal of crops, have not been faced with the need to make frequent moves to greener pastures. They have been able to become expert farmers, and industrious business people and government employees. The nomadic people remain largely as wanderers since they must cater to their herds' constant needs. The coastal Kenyans have, until recently, concentrated on occupations related to fishing and trading with foreign nations at their ports.

Kenya's excellent climate is a major attraction, along with the wildlife, which brings thousands of tourists each year and with it foreign currency for the country's economy

The Kiswahili Language in East Africa

Kiswahili is the recognized national language in Kenya and Tanzania since the two countries became independent. It is also widely spoken in Uganda and Zaire, and more recently has spread into other central and southern countries such as Angola, Zambia, Zimbabwe and Mozambique. It is the mother tongue of a group of people along the East African coast and the islands inhabited by the Swahili people. These people descended from members of many nations who came to trade along the East African coast as early as 1600 A.D. — Arabs, Portuguese, Persians and Europeans. Kiswahili is a combination of several languages, including English, and is very easy to learn.

In Kenya and Tanzania, Kiswahili is used in broadcasting, publications — books, magazines, journals, newspapers and written correspondence. It is spoken in official public addresses and used in some curriculum at lower grades.

Kiswahili is not generally spoken in tribal homes in rural areas. In urban areas however, more and more Kiswahili is used by those who come from different tribes. The average Kenyan speaks his or her vernacular in the home, uses Kiswahili in market places or when interacting with a different tribal member. English is spoken in schools and office settings.

As for tribal languages, there are over 40 ethnic groups in Kenya alone who all speak different dialects. It is quite common for Kenyans to speak more than a few different dialects in addition to Kiswahili and English. Since different languages are nothing out of the ordinary in the East African culture, introducing foreign languages is encouraged in schools, because East Africa is involved in foreign trade with countries all over the world. The most commonly studied foreign languages in Kenyan schools are French, German and Italian. English and Kiswahili are required language subjects in high schools in Kenya.

Swahili Words ... a visitor to East Africa will find useful when trying to communicate in Kiswahili.

Here's How the Vowels Sound:

a	as in man
e	as in men
i	as in pin
o	as in hope
u	as in Uganda

Bicycle	*Baisikeli*
Brother	*Kaka*
Bus	*Basi*
Car	*Gari*
Come	*Njoo*
Church	*Kanisa*
Father	*Baba*
Food	*Chakula*
Freedom	*Uhuru*
Hello	*Jambo*
How are You?	*Habari*
I want	*Nataka*
I don't want	*Sitaki*
Let's pull together	*Harambee*
Me	*Mimi*
Money	*Pesa*
Mother	*Mama*
No	*Hapana*
Please	*Tafadhali (Tafathali)*
Road	*Barabara*
Shilling	*Shilingi*
Sister	*Dada*
Thank you	*Asante*

Taxi	*Taksi*
Time	*Saa*
Toilet	*Choo*
Us	*Sisi*
Very much	*Sana*
Water	*Maji*
Welcome	*Karibu*
Well	*Nzuri*
What is the time?	*Saa ngapi*
Where	*Wapi*
Who	*Nani*
Yes	*Ndio*
You	*Wewe*
You (plural)	*Nyinyi*

To learn more Swahili:

    Teach Yourself Swahili — by D. V. Perrott
    Hodder & Stoughton, Ltd. Great Britain
    Or you can go to Google.com to learn more Swahili

What's in a Name?

Semantic Differences

American	British
Excuse me	I am sorry
Elevator	Lift
Two weeks	Fortnight
Ride	Lift
Recess	Break
Pressing	Ironing
Apartment	Flat

Call	Ring
Diaper	Napkin
Napkin	Serviette
Baby Buggy	Pram
Guy	Chap
Bracelet	Bangle
Get off	Alight
Purse	Handbag
Wallet	Purse
Peanuts	Groundnuts
Cookies	Bisquits
Candy	Sweets
Toilet	Water Closet
Resume	Vitae
Football	Soccer
Tuition	Fees
Grade	Class
Grade School	Primary School
High School	Secondary School
Diploma	Degree
Raisins	Currants
Glasses	Spectacles
Gasoline	Petrol
Rubbing Alcohol	Spirit
Bandaid	Elastoplast
Dinner	Supper
Hamburger Meat	Minced Meat
Basketball	Net Ball
Patio	Veranda
Pill	Tablet
Full	Satisfied

Top: Chwele youth making clinic furniture
Bottom: Chwele children cleaning clinic grounds

How to Use This Book

African people rarely consult recipes for their meal preparations. Cooking is an art — cooking without measurements — mostly acclaimed by women. In my tribe, a newly-married woman who does not demonstrate cooking skills — especially for the staple foods like *Ugali* — may be sent back to her family for additional training. No family ever wants their daughter to be returned to them for lack of simple cooking skills. The bride's family members always make sure that the young woman is a good cook before she gets married. There are no written recipes included in the list of ceremonial marriage gifts.

This book is written to encourage readers to experiment with African foods in their homes. I hope the recipes will evoke the reader's own culinary creativity.

First try the original recipe then create your very own "African" dish by omitting or adding desired ingredients when appropriate. Recipes in this book can be prepared for:

- potlucks.
- multi-cultural exchange celebrations.
- wedding celebrations.
- birthday celebrations.
- anniversary celebrations
- ethnic and multi-cultural curricula in schools.
- a healthy hearty African meal.

Certain methods of cooking have been modified to promote healthier food habits: instead of boiling vegetables, steaming is recommended when possible.

The recipes which meet the American Heart Association guidelines are marked with ♥.

Most of the ingredients can be found in regular grocery stores if you live in a fairly large city in the United States. Some of the ingredients may only be available in specialty stores which cater to African, Caribbean, Indian, Spanish or Asian clientele. In Canada and England most of the ingredients may be available in specialty stores only. In Kenya, all the ingredients are sold in open markets. Some of you — your friends or relatives — may even grow some of the plants in your garden.

Benefits of this Book

Proceeds from this book support Chwele Community Developement in Western Kenya. African dinners support Chwele Community Development as well as local projects through schools, churchs, and other special organizations.

This book:

- serves as an intercultural information reference resource to African-American communities all over the United States.
- is an additional resource on African culture to the existing but limited information in ethnic school curricula throughout America.
- serves as an important source of information to the young, lay and student populations throughout Africa, as well as preserving African tradition for future genera-

tions. Some Africans are no longer experiencing the same family support outlined in this book due to the changing family structure in Africa caused by urbanization and other elements of change. Africa is mainly an oral society. For centuries, traditions and customs were handed down from generation to generation by mouth. Times are changing and like other parts of the world, Africa is fast losing its traditions.

- provides basic nutrition information encouraging the reader to develop healthy eating habits.
- invites the reader to experiment with different foods from other parts of the world. Food has always been a common denominator in global relationships. Learning about the different "tastes" of another culture more than likely heightens the interest to know more about that country through travel, reading or interacting with people from that culture.
- exposes the reader to palatable dishes through the use of herbs and spices.

African Women and Food

The subject of food in Africa is synonymous with the role of women in that culture.

Although the vital contribution to food production by women in Africa is routinely overlooked, the awareness of their role in countries with poor economies has increased since the beginning of the United Nations Decade for Women in 1975. This issue was addressed with more emphasis when the Second World Women Conference was held in Nairobi, Kenya in 1985, and was taken up again in 1995 at the Third Decade Conference in Beijing, China.

In Africa alone, women account for 80 percent of the agricultural labor force according to United Nations statistics. In situations where men have moved to the cities in search of work, rural women have been left without help for carrying water, fetching firewood, clearing land, sowing, weeding and harvesting crops. On top of growing the food for meals and preparing them, women rear their children and attend to the chores in their homes.

Through the colonial period (from early 1900s to late 1950s), African women were denied formal education. In more recent times, developmental aid projects have been initiated by women's self-help groups *(harambee* groups) as well as the government to help meet family needs for clean and accessible water, replenishable sources for fuel and energy-saving devices such as improved cooking stoves.

Despite the heavy burden on the African woman, she is blessed with a boundless spirit of hospitality that is cherished in the community and throughout the African society. She is the thread that holds the African cultural fabric together. Family bonding and support enable her the strength to carry on, even at the worst of times.

The visitor who is fortunate enough to experience the African family circle and share what people offer so generously — no matter how desperate the circumstances — will have gained an enduring lesson in giving the most precious gift of all, the gift of self.

When the African woman prepares food, she always cooks more than her family requires, because neighbors, friends, extended family or even a stranger are likely to drop in during meal time. If you find an African family eating together, you are expected to join in the celebration of sharing.

I enjoy sharing African foods and recipes with my friends and neighbors. I hope that you use this book and these recipes in the spirit of the discovery of new foods and giving of self.

Cooking Methods in East Africa

Refrigeration is not available in rural areas in East Africa. Meals are prepared daily, fresh from the garden or purchased at the open market. Most of the rural families still use the three-stone cooking method to prepare their meals.

Three medium-sized stones are placed in a hollow in the ground, forming a circle. Firewood is piled in the center and lit. The cooking temperature is controlled by the amount of wood added to the crackling fire. The *sufuria* (deep sauce pan) is settled firmly on top of the tree stones over the flames. The smell of the wood fire and the aroma of the simmering food permeate the air with tantalizing results.

When the British came to East Africa they introduced wood stoves with ovens, which were followed by gas and electric stoves in the urban areas. During that time kerosene and paraffin contraptions were being used, and the invention of the *jiko* — a brazier — became a popular cooking convenience. The *jiko* is fueled by charcoal made from wood and is still being used for cooking in both urban and rural areas.

In many ways, life is still quite simple and uncomplicated by buttons and dials of sophisticated equipment in East Africa, which seems to fit the character of the small communities quite well.

In my own automated kitchen in Portland, I appreciate the convenience of pushing buttons, getting instant heat to cook our meals, heat the house, cool jugs of milk, wash our clothes and be "climate-controlled." But at times it seems artificial and sterile.

I miss getting down on my knees to tend the dying fire that glimmers between the smooth surface of the time-tested cooking stones. I miss the pungent smell of the rich, dark earth, and the roasting of green maize during the evening, in the warm presence, the chatter and the laughter of my family.

I remember how my brothers and sisters taught me to count with the help of the grains of maize as we ate them. It was a delightful way of learning for me, because it was associated with "eating."

Most of all, as a woman now, I miss the camaraderie, the story-telling, the laughter, the tears, the exchange of ideas and the benign gossip that took place in the Kenya kitchen of my youth. Now, I cook with my daughteres, neices, friends and my sister. We use the time to talk about life's challenges, joys, friends, growing pains and family matters. I love to cook with others.

Family Background

My love and appreciation for cooking stemmed from the influence my own childhood family exerted. I come from a large family of twelve siblings (six girls and six boys) of whom I am the youngest. Three brothers and one sister are deceased. In the African culture, the youngest child holds a special place in the family, and is the recipient of a lot of affection from everybody in the clan. Superstition or not, it is sometimes believed that the youngest child has certain special powers. In my sub-tribe, the youngest child is known (not incorrectly) as *Mutua,* meaning the "womb locker." All my brothers and sisters call me by *Mutua* instead of Grace.

Home was a large, multi-room, thatched farmhouse in the village of Chwele. After my parents died I went to live with my sister, Nora and her husband in a roomy, modern permanent house in the village of Chesikaki. That big house has been donated to the community and now serves as a reconciliation center and clinic. During my high school years, I lived in Nairobi, but always returned home for the school holidays.

Since I am the youngest, I saw only one of my four grandparents. My maternal grandfather known as Njunukha was still alive. He had fought in the First World War for the British against the Germans, and was over 100 years old when he died in the early sixties. My mother was his *Mutua* and he loved her immensely. For years he told us stories from the big war and the part of the world we had not seen. There was a deep bond and love between us.

My parents, Joel Wekhui Wasilwa and Maria Muyoka Njunukha died in their mid-fifties when I was about eight years old. My father was born about 1902 and died in 1956. Six years later, my mother, who was born in 1904, passed away. My parents were among the first generation of Africans to become Friends (Quakers) — who, by the way, were one the first groups to speak out and act against slavery in America.

My mother and father were always actively engaged in community affairs, and through Friends learned about the values of a Western education. They learned how to read and write, were looked upon as leaders, and mentored not just their own offspring but all the children in the community in the important values of becoming concerned and responsible adults.

Joel Wasilwa was a many gifted and innovative man. He was a tailor, a carpenter, farmer, teacher and soccer coach. (two of his students married my two oldest sisters.)

He was a popular coach because he taught traditional values and ethics along with soccer rules. He had to do a lot of things in order to be able to send his children to school. He owned a maize grinding machine, an ox cart and plough and established a co-operative organization for selling cash crops. He was tireless in his efforts encouraging his clans-people to send their children to school. In 1952 my oldest sister became the first trained and qualified, female teacher in our village.

My mother was a remarkable person as well. She was one of the best farmers in our area. She had a golden touch with everything that grew in the earth, she raised the best vegetables and the most flavorful herbs. On the land around our home, we grew lemons, oranges, *grandilia* (passion fruit), guavas, coffee, maize (corn), beans, millet, sorghum, sesame seeds, groundnuts (peanuts), *cassava* (yucca), sweet potatoes, pumpkins, Irish potatoes, bananas, squash, cabbage, kale, *sukuma wiki* (collard greens), onions, cowpeas leaves and several other varieties of African wild vegetables all year round. My father also kept a bee hive in our homestead and everyone enjoyed the fragrant, golden, sweet taste of honey.

Mother was an exceptionally gifted cook and housewife, and an exemplary mother to her own children as well as a mentor to countless children of the community. There was always plenty of food in the house and she saw to it that no one in the circle ever went hungry.

Since my mother lived longer than my father, I developed a special bond with her. She sang to me every day and carried me on her back almost all the time until I was about five years old and had grown too big and heavy for her.

She had a highly developed gift for counseling, the ability to settle squabbles, spent endless hours helping people reconcile their differences, and made the act of forgiveness a virtue. She passed on her qualities to everyone she raised and mentored. My parents were the light of my life, and I only wish I could have had them longer.

I was raised by my oldest sister and my brother-in-law, Nora and John Musundi, who sacrificed many of their needs for the sake of my welfare. They sent me to the best schools they could afford, and gave me a structured set of values for life. My other older brothers, sisters and their spouses helped raise the rest of us too.

Taking care of the young ones by the older siblings is a common practice in Africa which again is the result of the strong family ties, a set of indisputable values and a sense of tradition — all of which are faithfully practiced in daily living. Even though I was quite young at the time of my parents death, I had already learned the value of hospitality from them, and later on, from the rest of my large family.

My parents welcomed, fed and hosted extended family members, friends, students and strangers in our home daily. My mother was known near and far for her "Mother Theresa" virtues. The door to our home was always open and preparing food was one part of welcoming and caring for visitors as well as the family.

I had so many fine teachers in my life, and am grateful to all of them. My sisters, sisters-in-law and one particular niece, Nekoye, Judge Ruth Sitati, who grew up in our home reinforced my understanding of the value of African hospitality. I observed our customs and had hands-on instructions for the preparation of food under their dedicated guidance. They taught me the innovative art of African cooking.

I learned to cook with a "pinch" of this, a "touch" of that and a "bit and splash" of this and that. I learned to judge the consistency of a stew by stirring it, and trained my sense of smell to tell me when things were "just" right.

My brothers taught me to appreciate nature, and from my three younger brothers I learned how different foods grow. They taught me the art of cultivating the land, and caring for the plants by hand with an African hoe. They showed me how to hunt birds in the wild with a *fandiri* (sling), and how to trap birds right outside our kitchen. When I tagged along with my brothers while they tended the small herd of the family cattle, I picked up the names of birds, insects, plants and wild animals.

My favorite winged friends were, and still are, those beautiful, exotic butterflies. I have always been fascinated by their brilliant hues and intricate designs. I loved to watch them flutter from flower to wild flower in a dance of swirling colors enhanced by the bright sunlight against a blue African sky. As a child, I saw my mother's heart in the splendor of a butterfly. I knew that she had the most beautiful heart on earth — the heart that gave out of love for everyone who was fortunate enough to know her. She was a woman of very few words but she could move mountains with her quiet acts of faith. I find myself as bound to her these many years later, as I was as a child.

One of my brothers, Amos, raised and tamed more than 20 doves which lived in my mother's kitchen. At home, the kitchen was in a separate hut a bit removed from the house, and one of my favorite places. The doves drove my mother nuts whenever she was cooking. I did not understand why she had so much patience with my brother. Now that I am a mother, I think I understand.

During the many hours I spent in the wild with my brothers, I smelled the fragrance of the beautiful flowers, touched wiggly insects, listened to the singing birds, the noises of big animals, the burbling sounds of the clean streams flowing through the land.

In awe, I witnessed the brilliantly blending colors of rainbows arching high above the earth after a warm drizzly rain and felt the cool breezes rushing down from the very top of Mt. Elgon and brush against my face. I learned to appreciate the magnificence of nature. Well, not everything, I never did like all those slithery, crawly snakes.

We spent a lot of time outdoors on the land, and ate our fill from many vitamin C-rich varieties of African wild fruits and berries. I liked being with my brothers and enjoyed that kind of life, especially since I didn't have their responsibility of watching the cattle. Our livestock was not only a source of food, but helped plough the land, and were traditional wedding gifts to family members starting out on their own.

I began grade school during the colonial period. During that era there were hardly any proper schools for African children in Kenya, other than a few missionary schools. At my first grade school, Kimabole, we had no classrooms for first and second graders. We had no books, pencils or note papers. Our classrooms were under the sweeping branches of tall trees. We wrote in the dirt with our index finger to demonstrate to our teachers what we had learned. In advancing grades, we used black slates and white chalk to practice our penmanship. Each student had one slate for all the subjects.

Because of my parents' commitment to eduction, I was exposed to a great deal of additional learning at home. By the time I was in sixth grade, three of my sisters had become trained teachers. One of my brothers, Javan (deceased), was particularly insistent on teaching me how to use the dictionary.

One evening, while helping me with my homework, he asked me to bring him "Michael West." I went to his bedroom to look for that person. I looked everywhere, even under the bed. I returned to my brother and told him that I couldn't find "Michael West."

Javan worked the issue a little longer, poking fun at me. He finally told me that the missing person was one of the authors of an English dictionary he owned. I trudged back to his room, located the big reference book and brought him his "Michael West." I enjoyed the way he introduced me to the dictionary, and have valued its contents ever since.

When Kenya became independent in 1963, President Jomo Kenyatta's priority for developing the country was to build more schools, and many of them were built by parents through the *harambee* projects. In Kenya, I also attended Chwele Girls' Primary School, Lugulu Girls' Boarding School, and Alliance Girls' High School. Later I attended Chiswick Polytechnic in West London, England for two years. Finally, I attended Portland State University where I completed majors in business administration and business education (undergraduate and graduate levels respectively).

While at Portland State University, Paul and I got married. We had two "miracle" daughters. Muyoka (Mary) named after my mother and Lutomia (Elizabeth) named after Paul's aunt. Muyoka weighed two pounds at birth and Lutomia even less — she weighed all of one pound and a half. Both young girls have visited Kenya four times and have the fondest memories of our families and the closeness of the family circle.

I am grateful for the wealth of my African heritage, my beloved parents, my early school days and the blending of a western education, life on three continents, with the values, traditions and the beauty of my homeland.

If I have learned anything — it is *Harambee!* — the *pulling together* of a few for the benefit of all.

Top: Chwele women celebrate official opening of clinic
Bottom: Namwela Secondary School assembly with
Portland, Oregon volunteers

The African Family Circle

In most of the world communities, the value of the family institution is recognized as the very foundation of civilizations. In Africa, family life is especially important to everyone because of the combined strength and support it holds for the individual.

In the Western culture, the term family refers to members of the immediate family. In the African culture family means grandparents, parents and children, uncles, aunts, cousins, brothers-in-law, sisters-in-law — the extended family. Each extended family is the major component of a clan. A clan stems from a sub-tribe which in turn is a part of a tribe (see chart on next page). There are about 40 sub-tribes in Kenya.

My family tribe	=	Luhya.
My sub-tribe	=	Bukusu.
My maiden clan	=	Bakhoma.
My married clan	=	Bakokho.

Each clan is considered to share the same blood lines. Marrying within the same clan limits access to a genetic variety which leads to a high degree of vulnerability of passing on hereditary diseases.

That is why it is critical for young dating couples to identify each other's clans before the relationship starts. Typical African parents from certain tribes (the first time a couple meets) upon meeting the "intended" immediately ask to what clan he or she belongs.

If one or the other is closely related to his or her respective clan by blood, the continuation of the courtship is generally discouraged.

Clan members usually relate to each other as if they come from the same nuclear family. Many of the sub-tribes use relationship titles to address family members in order to maintain mutual respect, especially for older family members.

Following is an example of my own sub-tribe:

Paternal uncle	=	father *(papa)*.
Maternal uncle	=	uncle *(khocha)*.
Paternal aunt	=	aunt *(senge)*.
Maternal aunt	=	mother *(miyi/mama)*.
Male cousin/brother	=	brother *(wandase)*.
Female cousin/sister	=	sister *(yaya)*.

These relationships contribute to the deep feelings of identifying with a family, and manifest in a strong sense of belonging. Belonging gives one a feeling of worth and honor, of being somebody and of being recognized as a welcome member in the midst of caring and loving people.

Children especially need the security of all encompassing circle of recognition, appreciation and affection. Those youngsters who go without that emotional shelter are looking for it in all the wrong places. They find it in the back alleys of humanity. Gangs and dangerous cliques become the substitute family, and, unlike a real family, those alliances most often end in tragedy. This is happening all over the world as the family structure of the past disintegrates and many of the world's children threaten to become the rubble of the future.

In my own clan, the demonstration of the traditional cultural respect is in the way in-laws of the opposite sex greet each other. They do not shake hands or hug when they meet, and keep a certain physical distance between themselves as they honor each other's presence.

Each relative is viewed as having a specific value in terms of his or her role in relationship to the rest of the family members, and is looked upon as an individual with specific gifts. Though each family member is respected as an individual, he or she is even more appreciated as being a part of the whole family team.

Extended African families are inter-dependent socially, emotionally and economically, and the children in the clan are disciplined, guided and loved by all the members. The children have the freedom to express their needs and concerns to any one family member with whom they feel most comfortable.

Sometimes, when parental patience runs out for a while, children can always turn to relatives for a breather who are only too glad to help out. Hence the saying, "It takes a whole village to raise a child."

The vast majority of Africans do not have a Social Security income, welfare subsidies, life insurance policies or pensions. According to the Kenya government statistics

(2007) only a small percentage of 31 million people are wage earners. Therefore the chain of responsibility is passed on to the next generation.

When someone depends on an older brother, sister or uncle for handling school tuition, the benefactor does not expect to have his money paid back. However, tradition requires the recipient to extend that same sharing to the younger members in the family who in turn will do the same.

You may ask just what the extended family circle has to do with African cooking?

It has everything to do with it.

The cycle of sharing begins when most African families gather in a circle to eat their meals.

Generally the women prepare the food together. During that time they tell their stories, discuss events, and give advice to each other. Meeting and working together in itself is a strong bonding process. Since African families are generally large, children are usually served their meals in a separate circle. In rural Africa today, the majority of families still eat in a circle, helping themselves to their portion from one big bowl or dish which has been placed in the center of the circle.

The tradition of the circle automatically trains children at a very young age to share with other family members. A child typically wants to eat until his hunger is satisfied. When there isn't enough food to go around, the children eventually learn to look out for each other. Learning to share food in the family circle affects the children's behavior in all the other aspects of their lives. They are able to look out for each other while playing, fighting, working, studying, etc. The adult family members set the example for sharing at meal time.

Traditionally, Africans do not drink alcohol to get drunk, but consider the gathering to join in a drink a purely friendly, social occasion. At an African drinking party the villagers sit in a circle and sip from long straws dipped into a big pot containing the customary brew. Between slow sips, they discuss life in general and philosophize about the aspects of living and dying. The elders lend their wisdom to the circle and teach their views on marriage, child rearing, and ethics to the younger people. If a person gets drunk, he is asked to leave the circle and is escorted home.

It's almost inevitable that during meal time a visitor drops in. Whatever food is left is shared with the drop-in. If the visitor turns down the offer to eat, then his motive for the visit is questioned by the family, and the moment can become quite uncomfortable. But customs in Africa are quite delicate, and when visitors are given the choice whether or not to eat, the gesture is not considered an invitation and the guests' declining is acceptable. In the event of a visitor bearing news of a family loss, his declining to eat is acceptable.

If the guest has a good reason for not eating and the family accepts the excuse as solid, she gets to take home a live chicken in place of the meal she would have shared otherwise.

Eating together is a genuine gesture of acknowledging one another. Meals can last for several hours, and during that time the family reinforces the sense of caring and sharing — which in turn strengthens the family structure, fosters kinship and a sense of belonging which then carries over into the community.

The act of sharing becomes as natural as breathing for everyone. I remember when I was about eight years old, one of my sisters gave me my very own new pair of shoes. True to the spirit in which I was raised, I immediately gave one shoe to my best friend who was my age and with whom I shared just about everything. My family was not aware of my generous act. One day after a heavy rain fall, one of my sisters asked me to put on my shoes and accompany her on an errand. I showed up at her side, ready to leave, wearing my one shoe.

She asked where my other shoe was, and with child-like innocence, I told her that I had given it to my best friend, Nanjala. I could tell she was upset but instead of getting angry, she had to laugh. She then explained to me that sharing was a fine thing to do, but there were certain things one can't share. Shoes must be worn in a pair — one shoe really doesn't do anyone any good. I did get my shoe back, but whenever my friend needed shoes, I gladly lent her mine.

At times when there isn't enough food to go around, the positive emotional interaction that takes place in the family circle during a meal makes up for the void. Food is a feast for the body as well as for the spirit. That is one of the several reasons, I believe, why so many Africans are not overweight. People rarely eat alone.

Meal time is synonymous with family togetherness. When settling down to eat in the circle, people are rarely in a hurry, because eating takes place when most of the work for the day is done. The family members are relaxed and at ease with each other. They appreciate the offerings of the table and enjoy their meal in a leisurely fashion. Nobody has his eye on the clock. Their level of relaxation is at a high which aids the natural process of digesting food because the body produces the right proportion of digestive enzymes.

A time-honored tradition that makes this family time special is the hand-washing process before every meal. Family members pour water over each other's hands and wash them with soap in a basin or large bowl. This custom creates an atmosphere of respect and honor between the two people involved in the simple ceremony. It is especially heart-warming and therapeutic for the person receiving the water. To gently pour water over someone else's hands says, "I care about you."

The next time you wash up before a meal, have a family member or friend pour water over your hands while you wash. See how it feels!

The bonding of the African family continues to grow as some family members get older. The elderly and the very young are especially close to each other and are the most valued members of society. The elderly always live in their homes with members of their extended family.

The oldest son usually doesn't move away from his father's compound. When the parents get too old to take care of themselves, the son's family takes over and looks after their needs. Dying is a very natural process for the elderly. Their life is never prolonged by artificial measures for any reason. In fact, quite often some elderly people in Africa prefer not to be hospitalized, and make their wishes known regarding family affairs before they die.

The most touching and at the same time intriguing element about the wishes of the elders is that they leave their special blessings, skills or talents to a specific member of the family — someone who has been extremely close to the elder. African people are careful how they treat their elderly. so that they be blessed at the time of the passing of an elder.

Several generations live together, and the elderly spend a great deal of time teaching the young the traditional ways of the clan. The elderly possess a storehouse of character-building stories, fine examples of adventure and mystery, peppered with words of wisdom all which they dispense to their attentive, young audience. Children and young adults alike honor and respect the older members of the family, seek their presence and build their growth and maturity on the lessons learned from them.

In my sub-tribe, the elderly and children often relate to each other as brothers and sisters because of our child-naming process. Traditionally, child naming is a privilege usually awarded to the oldest member of the paternal family. Babies are named after ancestors who have passed away — a custom which keeps the ancestor's good character alive. (Some tribes name children after living family members.)

Children are named after their grandparents but not after their parents. The children are awarded the same respect as their namesake. For example, if the child is named after her mother, she is addressed as "mother" plus the chosen name with exactly the same reverence one would give one's own mother.

The interdependence of the African family can be quite an economical challenge in this day and age to some of its members, but the overall strength of this cultural distinction overweighs the negative aspects of being "too" closely knit.

African Wedding

On a bright sunny morning, in Chwele, a village in Western Kenya, the mood is charged with excitement. The air is filled with jubilant sounds from the beat of the wedding drums, which send their joyful message far and wide. Streams of villagers arrive, colorfully dressed in garments ranging from bright rainbow hues to muted earth tones, blending harmoniously with the land and the wild, cheering flowers along the paths and roadsides.

The people follow the sound of the drums and the robust aroma of food cooking which leads unerringly to the homestead of the bride. Weddings are usually celebrated in the month of December, which is a hot and dry season, following the maize harvest. The bright sun gently releases rays of blessings. People's faces are bright with laughter and their spirits soar with joy. Brilliantly-hued, wild flowers reflect the generosity of nature and the vitality of life. The weather is comfortable and pleasant.

The groom approaches the village accompanied by his army of villagers like a conquering warrior. Indeed, he may have conquered the heart of the bride, but he has yet to win the vigilant hearts of the bride's villagers. Her people warn him of their wrath were he ever to mistreat their daughter, and they let him know they have brought her up the right way.

When a bride is given away in marriage, technically she is no longer a member of her birth family. She assumes the name of her husband's family and his clan. In spite of this transition, she is still looked after and protected by her blood relatives.

The bride remains discreetly tucked away in a quiet room where she is surrounded by honorable elder women of integrity, who skillfully pass on to her their age-old tidbits of marriage wisdom. . The secrets of true womanhood and marriage are faithfully handed down to her. She knows the ways of womanhood, her responsibilities as a wife which includes the art of cooking. The seeds of love and endurance are sown in her heart. She is truly blessed by the elders' presence and their dedication to the young woman. The bridegroom is instructed in the same way by the male elders.

When she emerges from the room to face the expectant crowd and eager groom in the long-awaited ceremony, she seems transformed. She is the reigning queen of the day. She has become a novelty to the children. She walks on a bed of fragrant, bright wildflowers to meet her man. The flowers are lovingly sprinkled on her path by the delicate hands and happy hearts of younger sisters and cousins.

In the meantime, the men and young boys busy them-selves with the final touches of the seating arrangements under a huge umbrella-like sycamore tree. To top the joyous mood, every kitchen in the bride's homestead simmers with delicious flavorful authentic cooking. Like busy bees, the women and young girls skillfully chop and peel, dice, braise and simmer, and taste the bursting flavors of chicken and beef curries, fragrant rice with ginger and groundnut (peanut), spicy sauce, sesame seed sauce, mashed bananas artistically wrapped in aroma-releasing banana leaves. What a picture!

A traditional wedding lasts for two days. On the first day, the festivities take place at the bride's home and the next day is spent celebrating at the groom's dwelling. These highly charged, intense events last from dawn through the night.

There is excitement in the air and the sounds of joyful visiting between the members of the communities. Among the traditional ceremonies, the gift-giving event is one of the most touching and memorable of the day.

The gift-giving song is performed by the circle of guests and calls upon different relatives — one group at a time. When the mother's side of the family is called in song to come forward and present their gifts, aunts and cousins form a joyful procession singing as they make their way. They offer their gifts in praise of the bride and groom. The gift-giving song continues until all the relatives have been called — an event that takes hours.

Each group of relatives usually presents practical gifts according to the traditions of the culture. The bride and groom are given just about everything to start a homestead of their own — from cutlery, kitchen utensils, bedding, furniture to livestock.

In the Luhya tribe the wedding ceremony is never complete without the singing of the traditional song "Mwana wa mbeli ni Sikhoyelo" — "The first child in a family is a child of joy." This song casts a magical spell on the singers and they keep dancing on and on with seemingly inexhaustible energy. But the element that ties all the facets of this traditional wedding ceremony together, of course, is the wonderful food which has been so lovingly prepared and is so joyfully shared.

The love and care — the enormous emotional investment — that both the community and family expend on behalf of the young couple throughout their courtship and in their marriage, may well be the reason traditional marriages rarely break up, but thrive on the generous interaction between the young and the "old."

While we are on the subject of "old," I would like to mention just how much the East African community depends on the elders, how they are respected and revered. The old are the wise ones and rather than being considered a bother, they are the foundation of their clans' emotional and ethical well being, and the source of knowledge, traditions and ancient customs. The elders are indeed valuable. Without their guidance, new generations would go into the world with empty hearts and vacant souls.

Christmas Under The Sycamore Tree

A Special Holiday Gift

Holidays are special days and we celebrate them joyfully. But wherever we are, our thoughts always longingly return to home – especially at Christmas time. All I have to do is think of the giant sycamore tree and Christmas memories come flooding into my heart.

It is *Sikuku!* It is Christmas time in East Africa. The weather is sunny and hot. There is no blanket of snow that sparkles on trees and hills like in many other lands. December falls in the warmest and driest season of the year. The air is filled with anticipation and excitement of things to come. The heart of the village is jubilant and the people are filled with community spirit – *harambee!*

Every living thing awakens more fully as the dawn gets lighter and the sunshine becomes more brilliant and intense than at any other time. Birds chirp and chatter in the early morning hours as they witness the soft hues of the dawn blossom into a full-fledged, spectacular tropical sunrise. Young calves greet the morning with the low sound of their mooing eager to awaken their mothers to get ready for the morning feed and milking chores. The sunflowers seem to be laughing at the clear sky as they stand tall in the still morning air, the center of their golden halos rich with dark seeds.

Only the chickens appear a bit distraught and anxious as they wearily pick at the trail of white kernels of maize that coax them closer and closer to the kitchens – ready for swift hands to catch them. Some of the plump feathery chaps are quite wily and keep themselves at a comfortable distance from the treacherous fate that awaits them at the kitchen door. They seem to know their owner's delight for a fine meal of chicken curry.

Among the many tempting curries served during the holiday month, delicious chicken curry is everyone's favorite meal. A variety of traditional foods is prepared to accompany these mouthwatering main courses, among them *chapati, ugali,* rice, green bananas, sweet potatoes and vegetables in season.

Even though youngsters are given two four-week vacations during the year, schools close for six weeks during the Christmas season. Children who attend a boarding school return home for the holidays in time to help their families with the harvest. Compared to the lean seasons, during harvest time there is plenty of food for everyone. However, some of the crops are sold in order to meet the needs of school fees, the cost of books, uniforms and special treats.

This is the one time in the year when the children receive their traditional custom-made Christmas outfits, and the seamstresses in their shops barely have time to rest their busy hands. In my village, Chwele-Namwela most of the children show up proudly in their new finery for Christmas worship services. As in other parts of the world, some parents sacrifice much to be able to afford their children's new clothes — especially if they have several of them.

In my region, some people are affiliated with the Catholic Church or belong to the Salvation Army Church, but a predominant number are Quakers. As a young girl our Quaker congregation of many hundreds did not fit into the available church and worshiped under a huge, old sycamore tree at the Namwela Secondary School Campus. Like a giant umbrella, the ancient tree spread its enormous branches and provided welcome shade in a deep and spacious circle which also hosts many school activities. The ground around the tree is sculpted to form a rise that serves as a podium.

Our Christmas worship services are memorable and last from ten o'clock in the morning to four o'clock in the afternoon. The air is filled with joyous melodies from several church choirs in the area. The congregation joins in favorite carols sung in Luhya and Swahili, which ring out the celebration of Christmas Day. Our family used to be one of the several "singing families" who offer their gifts of song to the service. The congregation presents gifts to the participating choirs in gratitude for their efforts. The Christmas message is conveyed in a variety of ways, but overriding all the talks and all the readings are the songs – praising God and rejoicing in the birth of Christ.

Christmas time in East Africa is a time for families to reconcile their differences and celebrate the season. Christians, of course, rejoice in the birth of Christ and cling fast to the true meaning of the holiday. This is the time to strengthen the family and community spirit of togetherness and renew traditional values and customs — like story telling. Families use this time to reflect on and examine some of the traditional values which have been the backbone of their culture in the past.

The exchange of material gifts as it is known in Western cultures is hardly part of the East African tradition in rural areas. However, commercialism is quickly showing its face in urban life. As in most countries, the rural areas are slow to accept the newer ways and remain steadfast — for a while at least. When I was a young girl, gifts were of the heart and were shared from "heart to heart." These gifts were treasured, after all, that's all we had to give. But the gifts reinforced the feeling of being cared for and boosted our sense of self confidence. Gifts from the heart last longer than anything you can buy.

However, for material gift-giving we give something from our possession — perhaps a piece of cloth *(kanga)* or food. With that gesture, those who give the gift, share part of themselves with the recipient who values the treasure as much as the relationship. Just think what an effect this gift would have on a friend or loved one.

Instead of buying material gifts for your friends and family members, try one of these "heart-to-heart" genuine articles instead:

- Take time out and write a letter or a poem expressing your appreciation for that person.
- Share a valued personal possession with someone.
- Give a gift of time. Take time off from work or a daily routine and with intent and thoughtfulness share that time with someone who needs a friend. Do something wonderful with that person that will become a lovely memory.

- Purchase a telephone credit card for a friend or family member who cannot afford to keep in touch with you.
- Help out where you're needed; shovel snow or do gardening for a neighbor, cook for a sick friend, help … share … help and share some more.

Give from your heart the gift of "heart-to-heart."

I know you will have many other ideas for giving from the heart to fit the occasion and the needs of a grateful recipient. In the meantime, take all the monies budgeted for your usual purchase of Christmas gifts and give the amount to a needy family — for heat, clothing or food which they wouldn't be able to have otherwise.

When we were raising funds for Chwele Health Clinic in 1999, one of my friends, Sue Hildick of Portland, Oregon asked her family to gather their Christmas gift monies and give them to the clinic fund instead of buying gifts for each other. I will never forget the trouble she went through to deliver those precious gifts to me. We both worked for Oregon Health and Science University in Portland. One stormy, icy morning after Christmas, when it seemed like no one else had made it to work, I was at my office when Sue called and said she wanted to stop by. The roads were icy, dangerously slippery and I tried to discourage her not to venture out because I had taken some falls during this particular ice storm.

Sue was determined to see me that morning and arrived at my office all bundled up against the cold with love in her embrace and love in the smile on her face. She handed me an envelope and said that this was a Christmas gift from her family to Chwele Health Clinic. She represented her family with a grand gesture of honor of giving. The envelope contained more than $600 and a letter from Sue to her family asking that they adopt Chwele at this particular Christmas. Sue's dedication truly touched the deepest core of my heart. I embraced her with tears of joy, knowing that the gift would go a long way changing the quality of life in my village by providing better healthcare.

Sue had previously championed the fundraising process in 1998 by bringing Senator Mark O. Hatfield on board for this project. He was joined by Oregon Senator Avel Gordly in these efforts. They both later joined the Harambee Centre Advisory Council when the non-profit was incorporated in 2001 and are still active. Sue was a board member for two years. Giving and sharing where the need is the greatest brings hope into the lives of those less fortunate and may just give them a new lease on life — at Christmas time and any time.

When the Christmas worship ends, people slowly leave the protective shelter of the sycamore three — our outdoor church. Families join together, sharing in the gifts of love, laughter, food from kitchens of their hosting families and the celebration continues in the African family circle. It was indeed a day to cherish, a time to remember, especially for young children.

Negative reports about African conditions constantly reach the western world and often leave a biased and frightening image of that continent. However, because of the increased personal interest through grassroots projects like Chwele Health Clinic, these reports sometimes end up motivating some people to dig in and help. And they help in small ways and in big ways. The building of a medical clinic in my village is the result of just such care and generosity.

The stories you hear about Africa's problems — poverty, disease, depravation, political instability and economic problems are increasing mainly because the continent of Africa is racing against time with the pandemic of HIV/AIDS and its effects on her people. According to UN statistics, the life expectancy in most of Africa has dropped to the ages of people between 40s and 50s. There are more than three million HIV/AIDS orphans living in Africa today with no one to take care of them except they themselves and their grandmothers. Despite all this, there are some positive and wonderful things about my homeland. African people are a resilient and joyful people when circumstances allow. The joy has its roots in the act of sustaining traditional values. This feeling rests in the loyalty to community and family and an abiding faith in God.

With my writing I wish to bring you closer to the heart of Africa and the joy of the family circle despite the difficulties.

I wish you all wonderful "heart-to-heart" seasons of giving and sharing, and may these words inspire new strength in your family circle and bring you together in new love and peace for Africa and your family under a sycamore tree of your own.

Asante Sana!

Top: Lewis and Clark College students with Chwele children
Bottom: Chwele children give thumbs up

Kwanzaa — A Celebration

Kwanzaa is a seven-day holiday and was introduced to the United States by Dr. Manlana Karenga, founder and chairman of the Black Nationalist Organization "U.S." *Kwanzaa* is a cultural holiday recognized by African Americans to demonstrate the concept of the Seven Principles *(nguzo saba)* which are based on the African family value system. The meaning of these principles was taken away from African Americans by the ordeal of slavery, and colonialism further eroded African principles. They are now being recaptured to give these people (especially the children) a sense of positive African values.

The word *"kwanzaa"* comes from the Swahili word, *kwanza,* which means first and is part of the phrase *"matunda ya kwanza"* (first fruits). The biggest cultural celebrations in Africa usually happen around harvest time when there is plenty to eat and a time to give thanks for the harvests. The seven principles of *kwanzaa* stem from the "eating family circle."

Once one has learned the values of sharing and belonging through the eating circle experience, then one is able to more fully participate in the seven principles with a heightened community spirit and a sense of unity. One of the *kwanzaa* symbols is *zwadi* which is a Kiswahili word that means "gift." The giving of gifts part of the celebration is the highlight for the children. In traditional Africa, materialism did not exist, even at Christmas time. Since there was so little to give in terms of material gifts, African families gave to each other in many different ways. They still give of themselves to each other every day because that is all they have at times.

When an elder tells a story to a child, he blesses that youngster with memories no one can ever take away. When certain words of wisdom are used to demonstrate a cultural value to a child, that too is a gift he'll have forever. The time the elders spend with the young ones to teach them time-honored lessons of life is a great gift in itself. The time children spend making their own toys and dolls for each other is a gift. The most precious gifts are those of time, effort, sharing, encouragement, respect and belonging. During the *kwanzaa* celebration, children are encouraged to create their own decorations and gifts which symbolize cultural values to exchange with each other and not to expect to be given a gift as in the Western tradition.

The seven principles of kwanzaa are:

1. December 26 — *Umoja* (oo-moe-jah) Unity.
   To strive and maintain unity in the family, community, nation and race.

2. December 27 — *Kujichangulia* (koo-jee-cha-ngoo-lee-ah). Self Determination.
   To define ourselves, name ourselves, create for ourselves and speak for ourselves, instead of being defined, named, created for, and spoken for by others.

3. December 28 — *Ujima* (oo-jee-mah) Collective Work and Responsibility.
   To build and maintain our community together and to make our sisters' and brothers' problems our problems, and solve them together.

4. December 29 — *Ujamaa* (oo-jah-mah) Cooperative Economics.
   To build and maintain our own stores, shops and other businesses and profit from them together.

5. December 30 — *Nia* (nee-ah) Purpose.
   To make as our collective vocation the building and developing of our community in order to restore our people to their traditional greatness.

6. December 31 — *Kuumba* (koo-oom-bah) Creativity.
   To always do as much as we can, in the way we can, in order to leave our community more beautiful and beneficial than when we inherited it.

7. January 1 — *Imani* (ee-mah-nee) Faith.
   To believe with all our hearts in our people, our parents, our teachers, our leaders and the righteousness and victory of our struggle.

All of the symbols for *Kwanzaa* are:

- straw mat *(mkeka),*
- candle holder *(kinara),*
- seven candles *(mishumaa),*
- fruits and vegetables *(mazao),*
- ears of corn *(vibunzi),*
- gifts *(zawadi),* and
- cup *(kikombe).*

Celebrating one's culture gives one a sense of identity and the spirit of belonging. To appreciate what might happen in the future we need to know our past.

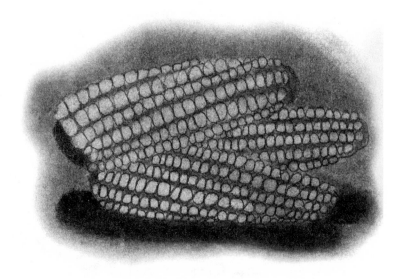

The Heart of Africa

Affectionate and kind is the African child,
While Africa's soul is both gentle and wild.
Women are born of a love that is strong,
Admired by men in words and in song,

She tackles her world with energy and drive,
And life around her never ceases to thrive.
She has little time for leisure and play,
But her spirit is happy, her heart is gay.
Singing like a weaver, she does her chores with a song,
And still has a smile when everything goes wrong.

Like an architect she builds her family foundation
Far beyond the horizons of her imagination.
Her life is dedicated to those she loves,
And the earth, the land and the song of the doves.
Her offspring drink deep from her cup of affection
And stand by her side in times of affliction.

Her magnificent heart embraces all things,
The flowers, the children and creatures with wings.
Her strength is the heartbeat of African life,
She's the teacher, the mother, the friend and the wife

She is the pillar of virtue in her African home,
The beacon of light for those who did roam.
She is a hundred times blessed with a sense of survival,
She is the vigor and the power behind value revival.
She is the soul and the backbone of true African living,
The real source of all caring, sharing and giving.

To my mother — *Asante Sana!*
Grace

Listing of Recipes

Main Dishes

Vegetables

Breakfast

Dessert

❤ = Meets the American Heart Association (AHA) guidelines.

Ugali
Maize Meal Mash

4 cups water
4 cups or less maize flour (yellow or white)

1. In a deep pan bring water to boil and reduce heat to medium high.
2. Using a flat cooking stick *(mwiko)* or a regular wooden spoon, slowly stir the flour into the boiling water a little at a time. Not all flour must be used.
3. Stir constantly to minimize lumping.
4. Keep pressing the lumps until they are all out.
5. Let *ugali* cook without stirring for about two minutes or so then turn it over.
6. Repeat this several times for about 10 minutes.
7. It should turn out as a soft, stiff dough.
8. Serve on a flat dinner plate and smooth the edges immediately with another dinner plate.
9. This is a difficult recipe because the consistency of this dish solely depends on the type of corn meal you use (course or fine). The finer flours tend to absorb more water as you cook.
10. *Ugali* should be eaten with a curry dish plus any vegetable.
    Serves six.

This dish is the most commonly used among all the staple foods in East Africa especially in Kenya. It is a stiff porridge. Africans generally do a lot of manual work and this dish is fairly high in calories to satisfy their hunger. After you eat *ugali,* you are not hungry for a very long time. This is an extremely popular dish among the Luo and Luhya tribes in western Kenya. The best way to learn to make this dish is to actually watch someone else do it first because timing on adding the flour is very critical. Nutritionally, *ugali* is a high-energy food — complex carbohydrate.

"If a new hoe needs to know the condition of the earth, let it ask the old hoe."

Ndizi
Mashed Bananas

10 almost ripe green bananas
2 cups of water
Pinch of salt (optional)
1/2 teaspoon margarine (optional)

1. Peel and wash bananas.
2. Chop each banana in fairly large pieces.
3. In a deep pot, bring bananas to boil in water and a little salt if desired.
4. Reduce heat to low medium and cook for 5 to 10 minutes until soft.
5. Drain all water.
6. Add margarine and mash bananas with a wooden spoon or potato masher.
7. Serve with curry and vegetable.

Serves four.

This is a popular staple dish in all of Est Africa — especially in Uganda and Western Kenya. It is a "light" meal for people who are not in excellent health, and is well liked by the elderly because it is easy to digest, and a good provider of potassium. In rural areas, bananas are mashed, wrapped in green banana leaves, and left to steep for a few hours near the cooking fire. With time, the leaves release their sweet aroma into the bananas. The result is a delicious treat. It is that special taste and aroma which makes *ndizi* a popular dish at wedding ceremonies.

Should you find yourself in an area in Africa where *ndizi* is prepared, don't miss the opportunity to try it because of its special aroma.

"Young birds don't know when bananas are ripe."

Ndizi Karanga
Fried Plantains

5 green plantains (almost ripe)
1 tablespoon curry
2 tablespoons flour
Pinch of salt
Oil for frying

1. Peel plantains and wash.
2. Dry plantains thoroughly with kitchen paper towel.
3. Slice plantains in in half crosswise then in half lengthwise.
4. Mix curry, flour and salt in a plastic bag. Add plantain pieces to bag and shake to cover bananas with mixture.
5. Heat a little oil in a frying pan. Fry plantains on both sides until brown.
6. Serve warm with curry dish and any vegetable of choice.

Serves ten.

Plantains are a popular traditional food. Fried plantains are mainly eaten in the urban environment, but are expensive because they are grown in rural areas and brought to the city by small peasant farmers who need money for children's school fees.

"Catch a bull by the horns, a man by his words."

Ndizi Na Mnazi
Bananas in Coconut

6 to 10 green bananas (almost ripe)
1 teaspoon margarine
1 large onion, chopped
1 medium tomato, chopped
Salt and pepper to taste
1 cup coconut milk

1.   Peel and slice (crosswise) the bananas.
2.   Saute the onion until tender
3.   Add tomato and sliced bananas and mix.
4.   Add seasoning, coconut milk and mix.
5.   Cook for 5 to 10 minutes until tender.

Serves ten.

Coconut is mostly used in cooking for added flavor by people who live in the coastal areas. Coconuts are fairly high in saturated fat and should be used sparingly in the daily diet.

Bananas are high in potassium.

"The person who isn't hungry says 'the coconut shell is hard.'"

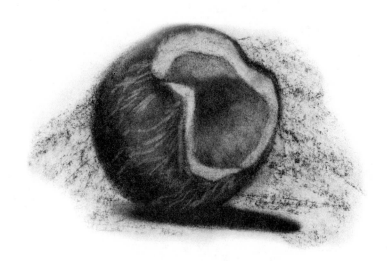

Wali Wa Tangausi
Ginger Rice

4 cups jasmine rice (white) or basmati rice
8 cups water
1/4 teaspoon salt (optional)
1 teaspoon margarine (optional)
1 teaspoon fresh ginger, grated
1 medium onion, chopped
1/2 teaspoon curry (optional)
1 cup boiled Valencia peanuts (optional) or
  1 cup boiled mung beans (optional)

1. In a deep saucepan, bring water to boil.
2. Wash rice.
3. To boiling water, add 1/2 teaspoon margarine, salt and rice.
4. On medium high heat, bring rice and water to boil then reduce heat to lower medium heat.
5. Cook until all water is absorbed.
6. When rice is about cooked, saute chopped onion and grated ginger in remaining margarine. Add curry if desired.
7. Add cooked rice (little by little) to onions and ginger and stir fry until rice is well mixed with ginger and onion, add groundnuts (optional) or mung beans (optional).
8. Serve hot with any meat curry or beans and a vegetable dish

Serves eight to ten.

This fragrant, delicious rice is prepared for guests and for weddings, birthdays, family reunions and other celebrations. Rice is used mostly in urban and suburban areas, and was first introduced to East Africa by East Indians and early traders along the coast. Brown rice is not readily available in East Africa because most of it has to be imported.

White rice contains small amounts of phosphorous, protein and potassium, and is nutritionally most beneficial when eaten with beans. Brown rice is more nutritious.

"Plant where you are and you will never be hungry."

Wali Wa Mnazi
Coconut Rice

4 cups jasmine rice (white) or basmati rice
8 cups water
1/4 teaspoon salt (optional)
1/2 tablespoon margarine
2 tablespoons grated coconut

1. In a deep pan, bring water to boil.
2. Wash rice.
3. To boiling water, add rice, coconut, margarine and salt.
4. On medium high heat, bring rice and water to boil then reduce heat to lower medium.
5. Cook until all water is absorbed.
6. Serve hot with meat curry or beans plus vegetable.

Serves eight to ten.

Since coconuts are grown in coastal regions of East Africa, their use is more common in that area. This is a delicious dish with a delicate flavor when properly prepared.

The nutritional value of rice is enhanced when served with beans.

"You will never pick a pepper from a lemon tree."

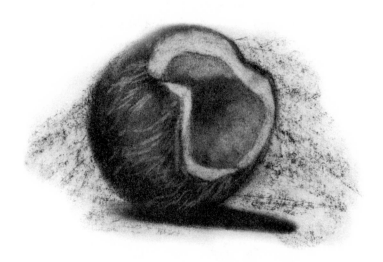

Viazi Kienyeji
Sweet Potatoes

4 large sweet potatoes
2 cups water
1/4 teaspoon salt (optional)
1 teaspoon margarine (margarine)

1. Peel potatoes and chop them in medium size pieces.
2. In a deep pan, put potatoes, water and salt.
3. Bring contents to boil and reduce heat to medium.
4. Boil until soft (10 to 14 minutes).
5. Drain all water.
6. Put margarine over all the potatoes and let it melt.
7. Serve hot with meat curry or beans plus vegetables.
    Can also be eaten cold with tea or coffee.

Serves eight.

Introduced by Portuguese traders, the sweet potato has been a traditional staple in East Africa for over 100 years. It is widely used, because it can be harvested in just three months after planting. Sweet potatoes make a tasty snack, a tasty side dish and can be served hot or cold.

Easy to prepare, sweet potatoes are an energy-producing food and rich in vitamin A.

"When the food is good, people are silent."

Samusa
Wrapped Meat or Vegetable Filling

1 pound ground beef or ground chicken or turkey or
  3 cups boiled mung beans for vegetarian
2 teaspoons curry powder
1/2 clove garlic, grated or pressed
Salt and black pepper to taste (optional)
1/2 bunch cilantro
1 medium yellow onion, chopped
8 ounces frozen French cut green beans, chopped
1 green pepper, chopped
1/2 medium size cabbage, chopped
1 cup cheese, grated (for tortilla wrapping only)
10 medium tortillas or 25 won ton wrappers
36 fluid ounces vegetable oil (traditional method)

1. Saute meat stirring frequently to prevent lumping. Saute until all visible fat is melted. Or saute mung beans.
2. Drain all fat.
3. Add seasonings. Add the vegetables, green beans and carrots first. Cook a little before adding the rest. Cabbage should be added last. Stir mixture together for next minute or so. Take off heat, cool contents and add onions and cilantro before wrapping

Contemporary wrapping method:
4. Spread 2 tablespoonfuls of mixture on 2/3 of a tortilla and roll. Sprinkle grated cheese on the remaining 1/3 of tortilla and complete rolling.
5. To melt cheese, place in conventional oven on warm (200 degrees) for 10 minutes or microwave for 1 minute. If refrigerated, microwave for 2 minutes or

in warm oven for 30 minutes. Small size tortillas are great for parties.

Traditional wrapping method:

4. In a deep pan heat vegetable oil.
5. Place 1 scant tablespoons of mixture on half of won ton wrapper diagonally.
6. Brush all edges with a little plain water. Fold won ton wrapper in a diagonal shape and press edges together until they are completely sealed. The wrapper should be dry on the outside before frying.
7. Deep fry in heated oil until golden brown. Remove from oil. Immediately drain on absorbent kitchen paper towel and let cool.

Samusa is consumed all over the world, and is known by different names. It is popular in India, the Middle East and in Africa. It was introduced to the East African region by people from India at the turn of the century. It is a favorite dish for natives and is enjoyed by western peoples.

The traditional wrapping method is used by Indians, Africans and Middle eastern people. A new wrapping method was created by the *African Women Harambee Association* of Portland, Oregon to accommodate people who no longer indulge in deep fried foods, and has been a hit. We discovered that this method saves a lot of preparation time and lowers the cost of ingredients.

Samusas are usually prepared for guests or for parties. Various size wrappers may also be used. This is a healthy recipe and a full meal in itself. Use as much of the vegetable mixture as you wish.

This dish is an excellent source of protein and carbohydrates.

Mchuzi Wa Kuku
Chicken Curry

1 whole chicken or
  12 thighs or drumsticks.
1 large onion or 1 bunch green onions, chopped
1 teaspoon garlic, grated or pressed
1 teaspoon ginger, grated
1 green bell pepper, chopped
1 can (8 ounces) cream of chicken or mushroom soup
1 heaping tablespoon curry powder
1/8 teaspoon black pepper (optional)
1 can tomato sauce (6 ounces) or
  2 large tomatoes, chopped.
2 cups water
Salt or seasoned salt to taste
1 can (8 ounces) coconut milk or
  2 tablespoons peanutbutter
1/4 teaspoon Italian seasoning (optional)

1. Cut up chicken, skin and wash.
2. In a deep pan, heat chicken in its own moisture.
3, Add onions, garlic, ginger, bell pepper and stir. Add curry and black pepper.
4. Add tomatoes or tomato sauce to chicken.
5. Add water and salt to taste.
6. Add either coconut milk or peanutbutter.
7. Add Italian seasoning and bring contents to boil and reduce heat to simmer.
8. Simmer chicken for 20 minutes or until cooked.
9. Serve hot with any of the dishes from main dish section plus vegetable.
   Serves six to eight

This is a special dish in most East African communities served at special occasions. Preparation of this chicken curry dish announces the fact that a special guest will be sharing the meal, or that there is a reason for a celebration. In the family circle, the guest always gets the largest choicest piece of chicken. This gesture signifies that the visitor is indeed the guest of honor, and is intended to make him feel acknowledged and accepted in the family's home.

You may add carrots and Irish potatoes to this dish to stretch it. If you add carrots and potatoes, add an extra cup of water during cooking because potatoes absorb more water as they cook

"Don't allow a hungry chicken to guard your corn."

Mchuzi Wa Nyama Ya Ngombe
Beef Curry

1 pound stewing beef or chuck roast, cut up
1 tablespoons vegetable oil
1 large onion or
  1 bunch green onions, chopped
1 teaspoon garlic, grated or pressed
1 green bell pepper, chopped
1 small bunch *dhania* (cillantro), chopped or
  1/4 teaspoon cumin seed
1 tablespoon curry
Salt to taste
1/8 teaspoon black pepper (optional)
1 can tomato sauce (6 ounces) or
  2 large tomatoes, chopped
2 cups water

1. Cut up beef and wash if need be.
2. In a deep pan saute onions, garlic, green pepper and cilantro or cumin seed. Add salt and pepper and curry.
3. Add beef to contents and stir thoroughly.
4. Add tomato sauce or chopped tomatoes and mix.
5. Add water and stir contents. If more liquid is desired you may add more water and salt accordingly.
6. Bring contents to boil and reduce heat to simmer. Simmer for 30 to 45 minutes or until beef is softly cooked.
7. Serve hot with rice or any main dish item and vegetables.

Serves six to eight.

The use of beef is not common in rural areas, and is considered a treat for guests and is used in celebration of special events, such as wedding, family reunion, dowry ceremony, etc. Sometimes the meat is dried over an open fire (barbeque) to preserve it for later use since there is no refrigeration in rural areas. Simmered in curry and spices, the dried variety is better tasting than fresh meat prepared in the same manner.

In order to stretch this dish, it is common practice to add vegetables such as *sukuma wiki* (collard greens) or cabbage in order to feed more people with the same amount of meat. Meat is a good source of protein, but since beef is rarely eaten, beans remain the main source for protein in the native diet.

"If you eat with a cunning person, hold a long spoon."

Mchuzi Wa Nyama Ya Ngombe Na Sukuma Wiki
Beef with Collard Greens

1 pound minced meat (hamburger meat)
2 bunches fresh *sukuma wiki* (collard greens)
1 bunch green onions or
  1 medium yellow onion, chopped
1/2 teaspoon curry powder
Salt or seasoned salt to taste
Pinch of black pepper
1 tablespoon peanutbutter

1. Chop and wash *sukuma wiki*.
2. Saute meat in a deep pan until all fat has melted from the beef.
3. Drain as much fat as possible out of the meat.
4. Add onions, curry powder, pepper and salt, stir. Then add *sukuma wiki*.
5. Stir thoroughly to mix and let cook for a couple of minutes.
6. Add peanutbutter and stir.
7. Bring contents to boil and simmer for 5 minutes.
8. Serve hot with *ugali* or rice.

Serves ten or more.

This is a dish most often prepared in urban and suburban areas. Minced meat is not available in most rural areas because the machinery for grinding the meat is not available. This recipe is an excellent way of stretching meat. Some families use more vegetables in this dish than suggested in the recipe. The end result is a vegetable dish flavored with a little minced meat which makes it a healthy meal.

You may replace beef with ground turkey or chicken. The collard greens can also be replaced with frozen or fresh spinach, or spinach combined with cabbage. Try different leafy vegetables for this recipe until you find your favorite.

This meal provides protein (depends on amount of meat used), fiber and calcium.

"A poor cook doesn't enjoy guests."

Mchuzi Wa Nyama Na Njugu
Meat with Groundnut Sauce

1 whole chicken
1 tablespoon vegetable oil for cooking
1 large onion, chopped
2 large fresh tomatoes, chopped
3 tablespoons tomato sauce (optional)
Salt or seasoned salt to taste
2 tablespoons peanut butter (groundnut paste)
1 to 2 cups water.

1. Chop, skin and wash chicken.
2. Saute onions in oil.
3. Add chopped tomatoes.
4. Add chicken and salt.
5. Add tomato sauce if desired.
6. Add peanut butter and mix all ingredients together.
7. Add water.
8. Bring to boil and simmer for 20 minutes.
9. Serve with rice or *ugali* or any carbohydrate main dish plus vegetable.

Serves eight to ten.

This is a more traditional way of cooking chicken in my country. Groundnut paste and *sim sim* paste (sesame seed paste) have been used as food flavoring in African cooking for many years. Since it takes time to prepare both pastes, they are considered a delicacy, and are used sparingly in some parts of East Africa. The oils from groundnuts and *sim sim* are the "good" oils which lower cholesterol in the body.

This flavorful dish contains lots of protein.

It is served at weddings as well as family and community celebrations.

"Don't plant groundnuts when baboons are watching."

Githeri Na Njugu
Beans and Peanuts

2 cups dried red beans
1/2 pound minced meat (hamburger meat) or ground chicken or turkey
1 large onion, chopped
1 teaspoon ginger, grated
1 teaspoon garlic, grated or pressed
6 carrots, diced
1 to 2 tablespoons curry powder
1/8 teaspoon black pepper
Salt or seasoned salt to taste
1 cup boiled groundnuts (peanuts) (optional)
  (boiled for 30 minutes or until soft)
3 cups sweet corn (maize)
1 can tomato or mushroom soup
1 can tomato sauce (6 ounce can)
6 to 12 ounces water

1. Soak beans in cold water overnight or for an hour in warm water before cooking time. Boil beans until cooked.
2. In a deep *sufuria* (sauce pan) saute meat and drain all extra fat out.
3. Add onions, ginger, garlic and carrots and stir.
4. Add curry powder, black pepper and salt and stir.
5. Add beans, groundnuts and sweet corn and stir
6. Add tomato sauce, soup and water and bring to boil.
7. Reduce heat to simmer and cook for 30 minutes.
8. This is a complete meal but may be served as a side dish.

Serves ten or more.

This dish is made in several parts of East Africa, and is prepared in a variety of ways and given different names. This recipe is the one most commonly prepared in Kenya, and represents the most staple dish among the Kikuyu and related tribes. Their version of this dish is made with Irish potatoes. This is a meal served in almost all boarding schools in Kenya. The school version is not as palatable as the home-made one because it is prepared in such large quantities and bears the stamp of institutional food.

The high school I attended is located among the Kikuyu people, and prided itself in having the best *githeri* cooks.

This wholesome, hearty meal is often eaten after a hard day's work, and does not require complementary side dishes. A bowl of *githeri* and fruit salad is all you need, since it is a great source of protein and carbohydrates.

"Even in time of famine, there is dew on the grass."

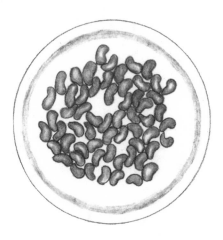

Mukenye
Beans and Mashed Sweet Potatoes

1 cup dried kidney beans
3 large sweet potatoes, peeled and chopped
Salt or seasoned salt to taste
1 large onion, chopped (optional)
1 cup maize (sweet corn)
1 tablespoon margarine
Water to cook

1. Soak beans overnight in cold water or for one hour in warm water.
2. Cook beans until very soft.
3. Cook potatoes in salted (optional) water until soft.
4. In a deep *sufuria* (sauce pan) saute onions in margarine.
5. Add beans and potatoes to onions. Add a little more salt if desired.
6. Mash potatoes and beans until well mixed and mashed.
7. Add sweet corn to contents and mix well.
8. Serve hot with vegetables. May be served hot or cold with Kenyan tea.

Serves ten or more.

Mukenye is a Luhya word for this dish, and is most popular among the Luhya people of Western Kenya. There are several versions of *Mukenye* due to the varieties of beans used in its preparation. It is often eaten for breakfast accompanied by tea or coffee — especially by young people. *Mukenye* is served as a side dish and is a good source of protein and energy. It is a traditional food, liked for its filling qualities after a hard day's work, and it is also a favorite snack.

"To ask twice is better than not understanding."

Maharagwe Meusi
Black Beans and Sweet Corn

2 cups black beans, dried
2 cups or 1 can (8 ounces) maize (sweet corn)
1 cup boiled groundnuts (peanuts)
  (boiled for 30 minutes or until soft)
1 tablespoon margarine
Salt or seasoned salt to taste

1. Do not soak beans, the earthy rich flavor gets diluted.
2. Check beans for debris and wash them.
3. Cook beans for 1 to 1-1/2 hour adding water as needed.
4. Drain all water out of cooked beans.
5. Add sweet corn and boiled peanuts.
6. Add margarine and salt to taste.
7. Mix contents thoroughly and leave on simmer before serving.
8. Serve hot with rice as a side dish.

Serves ten or more.

While this is not the most inviting looking dish, black beans have a most distinct, earthy taste people find hard to resist. Most people who frown at the look of those unappealing beans, change their minds once they have tasted them. It is one of my favorite bean dishes, and so easy to prepare.

Cook for recommended time or until tender.

This dish is a rich source of protein and potassium.

"Looking at food doesn't satisfy the stomach."

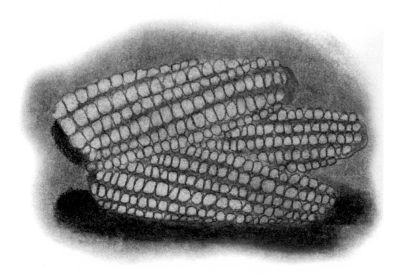

Mchuzi Wa Ndengu
Mung Bean Stew

2 cups dried mung beans
1 teaspoon margarine
1 large onion, chopped
2 medium fresh tomatoes, chopped
1 teaspoon garlic, grated or pressed
Salt or seasoned salt to taste
Pinch black pepper (optional)
1 to 2 teaspoons curry powder
1/2 cup water.
1/2 cup coconut milk
1/2 beef or chicken bullion cube
1/2 can cream of mushroom soup

1. Check beans for debris.
2. Boil beans in a *sufuria* (deep sauce pan) until soft.
3. While beans are cooking chop onions and tomatoes.
4. Drain all water out of cooked beans.
5. Saute onions in margarine then add tomatoes, cream os mushroom soup and all seasonings.
6. Add water, coconut milk and bullion cube, bring to boil and reduce heat to simmer. Add the beans and stir. Simmer for 3 to 5 minutes.
7. Serve hot with rice or chapatis.

Serves ten.

This is a delicious dish with a distinctive flavor. It is not commonly eaten in rural parts, but is a popular bean dish in urban and suburban areas. Many Americans have never seen or eaten mung beans, while mung bean sprouts are known and used among the American people. The bean itself is small and dull greenish in color. Mung beans cook much faster than other beans. You will find mung beans in health food stores or Asian markets.

Mung beans are known to have a richer supply of protein and potassium than some of their cousins. Their sprouts are rich in potassium.

"One who has eaten doesn't make a fire for the hungry."

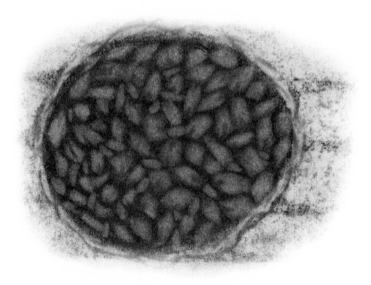

Maharagwe ya Kunde
Black Eyed Peas

2 cups dryblack eyed peas
I can sweet corn
1 small chopped onion
1 tablespoons vegetable oil
1/2 can (8 ounce) cream of mushroom or
  cream of chicken soup
1 can (6 ounces) tomato sauce
1 cup water
1 heaped tablespoon groundnut sauce
  (natural peanut butter)
1/4 teaspoon crushed fresh garlic or garlic salt
1/2 teaspoon curry powder
1/2 cube chicken bullion
Dash of Italian seasoning (optional)

1. Wash peas in hot water to soften them
2. In a sauce pan, pour hot water over beans until covered and boil on medium high for 15 minutes or until soft. Do not overcook.
3. Lightly sauté onions in oil, add chicken bullion and stir until melted
4. Add curry powder, garlic, and Italian seasoning. Stir
5. Add soup and stir until hot. Add groundnut sauce and stir until smoothly mixed
6. Add tomato sauce and stir well
7. Add water and stir well
8. Add beans and sweet corn, stir lightly and let simmer on low for 5 minutes.
9. Add salt as needed.
10. Serve with rice and cooked vegetable or salad.
    Serves eight.

This is a very popular recipe in many parts of Africa. It is especially popular in Kenya because the leaves from the black eyed peas are used as a favorite leafy vegetable called kunde in Swahili. It is commonly served with ugali, rice or chapati. This dish is also commonly served in the southern States of USA. I call this recipe a multi-purpose recipe because you can substitute the black-eyed peas and sweet corn with:

- Either 6 cups of chopped egg plant in the very same sauce (cook on medium. heat for 10 minutes)
- Or 2 pounds of chopped fresh mushrooms in the very same sauce (cook on medium. low heat for 5 minutes)
- Or 4 cups of chopped sweet potatoes (cook on medium. heat for 10 minutes or until soft)
- Or 4 cups leftover deboned chicken (simmer for 5 minutes)

Lentils

2 cups dried lentils
2 cups carrots, sliced
1 large onion, chopped
1 tablespoon margarine
1 teaspoon garlic, grated or pressed
1 teaspoon ginger, grated
1 to 2 teaspoons curry powder
Pinch of black pepper
Salt or seasoned salt to taste
1 can tomato sauce (6 ounces) or
   1 large tomato, chopped
12 ounces of water or less
1/2 can cream of mushroom soup

1. Check lentils for debris and wash.
2. Saute onions and carrots in margarine in deep pan.
3. Add seasonings.
4. Add lentils and mix.
5. Add tomato sauce or tomatoes, cream of mushroom soup and water.
6. Bring to boil and simmer for 10 minutes or until well cooked.
7. Serve with rice or *chapatis*.

Serves ten or more.

This is a typical East Asian or Mid-Eastern dish. It has been served in East Africa for so long that it is considered one of the authentic African dishes. It is mainly eaten in the urban and suburban areas.

Lentils have a distinct taste but are delicious and rich in phosphorus and potassium.

"A little axe can cut down a big tree."

Irio
Mashed Irish Potatoes, Beans and Vegetables

1 to 2 tablespoons margarine
6 to 10 large Irish potatoes, peeled, chopped
   and cooked
1 cup red beans, cooked
   (boiled for 30 minutes or until soft)
1 cup chopped carrots, cooked
1 pkg. frozen chopped spinach (10 ounces), thawed, or
   fresh spinach
Salt or seasoned salt to taste
1 cup or one can (8 ounces) maize (sweet corn)

1. Prepare and chop all vegetables.
2. In a *sufuria* (deep sauce pan) saute onion until soft.
3. Add potatoes and carrots and stir for about 5 minutes.
4. Add beans and stir.
5. Add spinach and stir.
6. Add salt.
7. Mash mixture thoroughly.
8. Add maize and mix well.
9. Let simmer for 3 to 5 minutes.
10. Serve hot with curry.

Serves ten or more.

Irio can be prepared in many different ways. The above recipe is only one of the several versions for this tasty dish which originated from the Kikuyu people who have perfected its taste. One of my sisters, Elizabeth, makes the best *irio*. When we visit with each other, she treats us to her famous version of preparing *irio*.

In the spring of 1994 she came to visit us in Portland. After the children had acquainted her with our city's bus system, she asked matter-of-factly what bus line would take her to Fred Meyer shopping center.

One evening we came home from work and were greeted by the most delicious, but familiar aroma. I was puzzled because I didn't have the ingredients for cooking *irio* in the house. But my sister simply had taken the bus to *Fred Meyer.* On her way back, she had gotten off two stops earlier than she should have since she was not familiar yet with our area. She had to walk the rest of the way lugging a heavy shopping bag — uphill all the way. She had cooked a surprise dinner for us, and served us her delicious *irio*. Her adventure of shopping by herself made the dinner even more special.

Irio is a good source of potassium and phosphorus. Pumpkin leaves can be used instead of spinach.

"Pleasantries and compliments are soon forgotten, criticisms and insults are long remembered."

Mandazi
Donut-like Fried Bread

4 cups all purpose flour
2 level teaspoons baking powder
2 tablespoons margarine
1/4 teaspoon *masala* (powdered mixed spices) or
   any one of the following spices:
   cinnamon, cardamom, all spice, ginger.
2 to 3 tablespoons sugar
1 egg
1/4 cup milk
1/2 cup warm water
Vegetable oil for cooking

1. Sift flour and baking powder together.
2. Rub margarine into the flour with finger-tips until smooth.
3. Add spice to flour and mix. And sugar to flour and mix.
4. Beat egg, milk and water together. Little by little add water mixture into the flour and stir slowly with a wooden spoon until you have a semi-sticky dough.
5. Knead dough with hands until it is smooth and not sticky (pizza-like dough).
6. Heat oil in a deep pan until hot. Test with a small piece of dough, if it cooks, then oil is ready.
7. Roll dough to 1/4 to 1/2 inch thick. Cut with dinner knife in desired sizes and shapes.
8. Deep fry in hot but not burning oil until golden brown.
9. Serve hot or cold with Kenyan spicy tea or coffee.
Serves ten or more.

Mandazis as we know them in East Africa are a universal food simply known by different names in various parts of the world. They are not a traditional food in East Africa, yet they have been around for close to a century. *Mandazis* are similar to donuts in the Western world. We prepare them less sweet and they are more chewy and drier in consistency. *Mandazis* can be made in different flavors, are eaten for breakfast, make a popular snack food and are quick to prepare.

Most East African families can whip them up in just a few minutes to accompany a cup of tea or coffee for unexpected guests. They are extremely popular with children and are mainly an energy food.

"Awe and wonder are everywhere, if you open your eyes."

Flaky Chapatis
Fried Bread

4 cups all purpose flour
1 cup whole wheat flour
Pinch salt
1 tablespoon margarine
1 cup warm water
Oil for cooking

1. Add salt to flour and lightly mix.
2. Add margarine and rub it into flour with finger tips until flour is smooth.
3. Make well in center of flour and pour in half the water. Mix slowly with a wooden spoon adding rest of water little by little until dough is firm but soft.
4. Knead the dough with your hands (adding a little flour if necessary) until it's smooth.
5. Divide dough in 10 balls. Roll each ball into a circle, rub the circle with a little margarine, fold from one end and roll it with your hands into a long layered piece of dough.
6. Stretch and fold it into a wheel-like shape.
7. Roll out each piece of dough into a circular shape (abut 6 to 8 inches diameter).
8. In a frying pan, heat a little oil, place circle in pan. Rub a little oil on top of circle. Cook both sides until golden brown in some areas.
9. Serve hot or cold with curry dish plus vegetable.

Serves ten.

Chapatis is a flat lightly fried bread made from wheat flour. This is an East Indian dish which was introduced to East Africa in the early 1900s. It is a popular dish among young people, and is a winner with every guest. It is mostly served in urban areas where wheat flour is more readily available. Because *chapatis* is fried in oil, it has lots of calories, and takes time to prepare. Chapatis are best eaten with mung bean stew (page 94) or black eyed peas (page 96) or lentils (page 98). Drink lots and lots of water after you have eaten *chapatis* to aid the digestive process. This is an energy food and has only minimal (other) nutrients.

"If you don't suffer, you won't gain wisdom."

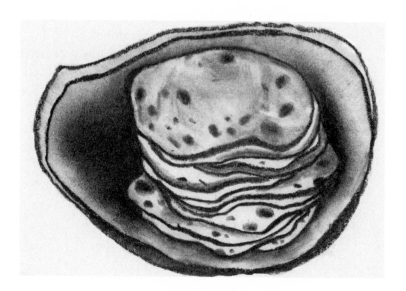

Mkate
Home-made Bread Rolls

1 package dry yeast
1/4 cup lukewarm water
1 egg
3 teaspoons sugar
3/4 cup hot water
1 tablespoon oil
1 teaspoon salt
1-1/2 cups all purpose flour

1. In a large bowl mix yeast with 1/4 cup water and stir until yeast dissolves.
2. Add the rest of the ingredients (except flour) into the bowl and mix well.
3. Add flour to mixture. The consistency of dough should be a little softer than pizza dough.
4. Divide dough into 8 equal parts and place on an 8 inch round oiled and floured pan.
5. Place on top of the stove and let it rise for 30 minutes.
6. Preheat oven to 350 degrees for 10 minutes before you start baking. Bake until rolls are golden brown, about 15 minutes.
Serves eight.

This recipe was shared with me 25 years ago when our family first met Nawanga Khalayi (Kathy Price). Nawanga came to live with us when we were expecting our younger daughter, Lutomia. I had to stay in the hospital for several weeks confined to complete best rest before Lutomia was born. Nawanga helped take care of our three-year-old daughter, Muyoka during my absence. She made these wonderful bread rolls just about every day, and always brought me a sample of her daily batch to the hospital, which meant so much to me.

She continued to bake these delicious rolls every day while I was recovering at home. *Mkate* literally became our staple food during that time. Nawanga lives in Tacoma, Washington now, but whenever we see each other, we break bread together — in the form of *mkate*. In July 1994, Nawanga traveled with us to our homeland, Kenya. She managed to arrive in Nairobi two days before we did. When we showed up at my sister's house where she was staying, she welcomed us home with a basket full of these wonderful rolls, along with freshly brewed, fragrant Kenyan tea. After having eaten air plane food, we practically inhaled the gracious offerings. It was a grand and wonderful reunion on Kenyan soil.

"You deserve what you serve."

Kabichi
Cabbage

1 medium-large onion, chopped
1/2 to 1 bunch green onions, chopped
1 tablespoon vegetable oil
1 medium head cabbage, shredded
1 teaspoon curry powder
Salt or seasoned salt to taste
3 carrots, shredded
1/2 bunch cilantro, chopped (optional)
1/4 cup half-and-half (optional)

1. Saute onions in oil.
2. Add carrots, stir and cook on low heat until vegetables look cooked. Do not over-cook.
3. Add curry and salt and stir well.
4. Add cabbage, turn for a few minutes until half cooked.
5. Add cilantro.
6. Add half-and-half.
7. Serve with any carbohydrate and curry dish.

Serves six to eight.

Cabbage is a universal vegetable and can be cooked in countless different ways. This recipe is one of many — in Africa alone.

This is one of the most popular recipes in the first edition which was featured on a local TV channel. It is a must-try recipe.

Cabbage supplies the body with fiber and vitamins. Research shows that cabbage is a possible cancer prevention food.

"Fine words don't produce food."

Sukuma Wiki Na Kabichi
Cabbage with Collard Greens

1/2 pound minced meat (hamburger) or
   ground chicken or turkey
1 medium onion, chopped
1/2 teaspoon curry powder
Salt or seasoned salt to taste
1 bunch fresh collard greens, chopped
1 medium cabbage, chopped

1. In a deep pan saute meat until all extra fat has melted
    off the meat.
2. Drain all the fat off of meat.
3. Add onions to the meat and stir.
4. Add curry powder and salt and stir.
5. Add collard greens and stir.
6. Cook, covered for 5 minutes at medium heat. Do not
    burn.
7. Add cabbage and stir until lightly cooked.
8. Serve with any carbohydrate and curry dish.

Serves ten or more.

This is one of the most commonly eaten combinations of vegetables in East Africa, and is served both in rural and urban areas. These vegetables are inexpensive and easy to prepare in a very short time. Meat may be added to improve the taste and nutritional value of this dish. This combination is generally served with *ugali* and rice, and is a good supplier of fiber and vitamin A.

"A hungry chicken wakes up early."

Okra

1/2 pound minced meat (hamburger)
1 medium onion, chopped
1/4 teaspoon fresh garlic, grated or pressed
1 teaspoon curry powder
1 package frozen okra (10 ounces) or
  1 pound fresh okra, chopped
2 large fresh tomatoes, chopped or
  1 can tomato sauce (6 ounces)
1/2 to 1 cup water

1. In a deep *sufuria* (sauce pan), saute meat until all the fat has melted off the meat.
2. Drain all the fat off of the meat.
3. Add onion, garlic and curry.
4. Add tomatoes or tomato sauce and stir.
5. Add the okra and stir well. As it starts to cook, it gets more and more slippery.
6. Add water and stir.
7. Cook for 5 to10 minutes. When it is cooked the consistency is runny and slippery.
8. Serve with *ugali* or rice and any curry dish.

Serves six.

Okra has a distinct and delicious taste. It has a slightly slimy consistency which some people may not care for, while others don't seem to mind. Since there are several other wild vegetables in Kenya *(murere, murunde, endelema,* etc.) which have a similar characteristic as okra, we are used to its peculiarity. In America I have seen okra used in casseroles — apparently to disguise its less attractive characteristic.

Okra is a rich source of vitamin A, and is mainly served in urban and suburban areas, as well as in the coastal regions.

"Walk carefully, your reputation follows you."

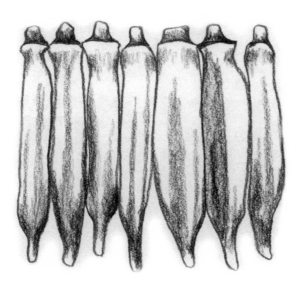

Kunde
Cow Pea Leaves

4 cups of *kunde* (cow pea leaves)
1/2 cup water for cooking
Salt or seasoned salt to taste
1 small onion, chopped
1/2 teaspoon oil
1/4 teaspoon curry powder (optional)
1/4 cup half-and-half or
   1/2 cup whole milk (optional)

1. Wash cow pea leaves thoroughly.
2. Saute onions in oila and add curry.
3. Add salt and cow pea leaves.
4. Cook on medium heat until tender, about 5 minutes. You may steam vegetable instead of boiling.
5. Add half-and-half or milk.
6. Keep on low heat until served within a few minutes.
7. Serve with *ugali* and curry dish.

Serves six.

Cow pea leaves are a traditional food in many parts of Kenya. Natives of Tanzania and Uganda consume the cow pea seed itself more than its leaves. In Kenya cow peas are grown more widely among the Luhya people. Due to the increased demand, it has become a costly vegetable in urban areas. In the rural areas it is more affordable but still less available that *sukuma wiki* (collard greens). Cow pea leaves are cooked in several different ways, but this recipe is the most commonly used.

Cow pea seed is available in Asian and Mexican stores in America, but the leaves may be found in the South. You may grow the pea in your garden during the summer. I have successfully raised cow peas in Portland. You may freeze the leftovers for use at another time.

Bean leaves may be used as a substitute.

This vegetable is high in fiber.

"When you take a knife from a child, give him a piece of wood instead."

Groundnut Sauce with
Spinach or Collard Greens

2 bags (1pound) of frozen leafy spinach
1 heaped tablespoon natural groundnut sauce (peanut butter)
Salt to taste

1.   In a sauce pan, heat spinach while stirring occasionally until it starts to boil.
2.   Add groundnut sauce and stir until well smoothly mixed.
3.   Add a little salt to taste if desired.

Note: You may use 2 bunches of fresh chopped collard greens instead of spinach if desired. You may also mix the two vegetables if desired.

Serves eight

This dish is easy and fast. It is best when prepared the last minute just before the meal is served. If you use spinach only, it takes about five minutes to cook. Collard greens are a very common vegetable in East Africa. It is eaten at least twice a day by most families in Kenya. Hence those who eat it frequently are generally in good health because of the richness in vitamins. Africans love to eat it with ugali or rice.

"Where there is no wealth, there is no poverty."

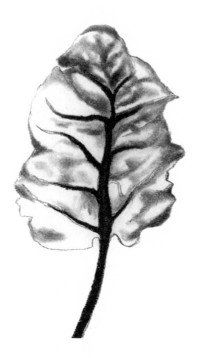

Uji
Porridge

4 cups water
1 cup cornmeal flour (yellow or white) or millet flour
1 cup milk (optional
Lemon to taste (if milk is not used)
Sugar to taste

1. In a deep *sufuria* (sauce pan) bring 3 cups of water to boil.
2. In a bowl, mix flour with 1 cup of cold water.
3. Add flour mixture to boiling water and stir constantly to avoid lumping. As the porridge cooks, it becomes thicker and thicker. When it starts to bubble, add lemon or milk, but not both. If lemon is used, substitute water for the cup of milk.
4. Depending on how thick you want the porridge, you may add more water or more flour/water mixture.
5. Serve with fruits and a protein food.
6. Add desired amount of sugar to each individual serving bowl because not everybody desires the same amount of sugar.

Serves four.

Uji is served at breakfast in every home in the morning, and is very simple to prepare. It is a popular food for babies, the elderly and is served to sick people who are unable to digest a heavier meal. *Uji* contains a generous supply of fluids which helps prevent dehydration in the body. It is nourishing and rich in calcium when served with milk, and can help meet the fluid intake requirements. It is mainly an energy dish. When lemon and milk are used at the same time, the milk curdles due to the acid in the citrus fruit.

"People who chatter to you will chatter about you."

Mayayi
My version of the commercial product
Egg Beater

1 dozen egg whites
1/4 cup non-fat dry powdered milk
1 tablespoon vegetable oil
2 drops yellow food color or
    1/8 teaspoon turmeric

1. Separate egg whites from yolks and throw away yolks.
2. Mix all ingredients in a blender or use a manual egg beater.
3. Pour into ice cube trays and freeze.
4. When frozen, remove individual cubes from tray and store in a plastic bag in freezer.
5. Cubes can be thawed instantly in a microwave or overnight in the refrigerator for breakfast the next day.
6. Use in cooking like any regular egg.

This is not an African recipe. It was given to me by a friend of mine, Loretta Thorpe of Portland. She inspired me with recipes and ideas that relate to "cooking for the heart." People concerned about their saturated fat and cholesterol consumption levels don't have to stop eating eggs. The egg yolk is high in saturated fat (1.7 grams) and also high in cholesterol, but the egg white has no trace of fat at all. It has a little calcium though. Eggbeater (trade name) products available in stores are more expensive than regular eggs. When making your own version of this commercial product, prepare it in large amounts and freeze for later what you don't use.

"If you wait long enough even an egg will walk."

Kenyan Mayayi
Scrambled Eggs — Kenya Style

6 eggs or 2 cups egg beater mixture
1/2 cup milk (if regular eggs are used)
1/2 teaspoon oil
1 small onion, chopped
1 cup carrot, grated
1/2 cup frozen peas or French-cut beans
1/4 teaspoon curry powder
Salt or seasoned salt to taste.

1. If regular eggs are used, beat eggs and milk together.
2. In a frying pan, saute onions, then add carrots and peas and seasoning.
3. Stir vegetables until about half cooked.
4. Add eggs or egg mixture and scramble.
5. Serve with bran muffins and lots of fruit.

Serves six.

Egg dishes are eaten all over the world. This recipe is a variation of how most Kenyans and other East Africans scramble their eggs. You may vary the kinds of vegetables used in this dish. This is a good way to consume your required amount of vegetables at breakfast or brunch.

Mayayi is rich in protein, vitamin A and calcium, and is ideal as a light meal when you lack time or energy for cooking. You may use this same recipe to prepare an omelet (without milk).

In Kenya this dish is served with rice or *ugali* to substitute for meat nutrients.

"The one-eyed man doesn't thank God until he sees a blind man."

Saladi Ya Matunda
Tropical Fruit Salad

1 small papaya
3 seedless naval oranges
1/2 ripe fresh pineapple
2 mangoes
2 ripe bananas
2 tablespoons coconut flakes (optional)

1. Wash all fruits before pealing. Using a sharp knife, peel all fruits, and cut them up in small pieces into a large bowl.
2. Add coconut flakes and lightly mix all fruit.
3. Cover bowl and let stand in refrigerator until time to serve.

Serves ten or more.

In Africa we don't generally eat desserts because our meals are heavy. We eat leisurely and take our time, and by the end of the meal, we are too full (satisfied) to eat anything else. However, whenever we serve dessert, it is almost always a fruit salad. In my humble opinion, fruit salad is the most ideal dessert for just about everybody. It is good for you, it is easy to prepare, relatively inexpensive if seasonal fruits are used, and it is low in calories and offers a full value of nutrients.

Fruit can be the dessert at every meal. I simply vary the fruits, and select ripe pieces when they are at their best.

Many of the desserts from the Western culture are delicious, but they are high in fat, sugar, have minimal nutrients, and often take a lot of time and expense to prepare.

Fruit salad or just regular fruits are my all-time favorite choice for dessert. Fruits are rich in vitamin C and vitamin A.

The most common way of eating fruit in Africa is peeling it (if necessary) and eating it the way it comes. Most Africans prefer hand peeled oranges to the knife-peeling method. Hand-peeled oranges supply you with more pulp which is better for the digestive system. Instead of putting a banana in a bowl and adding ice cream to it, just peel the banana and eat it plain. Eat as many varieties of fruits as possible.

"Don't try to carry water in a basket."

Machungwa
Orange Slices

4 seedless navel oranges

1. Wash and slice oranges, or hand-peel them.
2. Serve slices in a decorative fashion or break up the wedges and serve.
3. Eat with your (washed) fingers.

Serves four.

Oranges are a tropical fruit, and are a favorite dessert in my country whenever they are in season. Few fruits match the richness, flavor and generous amounts of juice this citrus offers.

"Fruit that isn't ripe doesn't fall to the ground."

Chai
Kenyan Tea

2 cups water
Pinch of ground cardamom
1/4 teaspoon of fresh cut ginger, grated
2 sticks cinnamon
1/2 teaspoon tea leaves
Sugar to taste (optional)
2 cups whole milk or 2% milk
6 drops vanilla

1. In a small deep pan, add spices to water and bring to boil.
2. Add tea leaves and immediately add the milk.
3. Cook on high heat until tea boils. Add vanilla. Watch it closely so that it does not boil over.
4. Sieve tea into pot and serve with snack or after a meal.

Serves four.

Tea is the second largest commodity of Kenya, (tourism is number one) and is the most popular hot beverage in East Africa — even in hot weather. There, you will often hear the cliche, "any time is tea time." This is true because any time you visit with someone, the first beverage you are offered is tea, while the meal is being prepared. Kenyan tea has a pleasant taste and flavor because of the spices used in preparing the drink, and with milk added, is nutritious and more satisfying, and becomes a good source of calcium and energy.

You will get best results with black teas from India, Sri Lanka, Kenya and English breakfast teas.

The additional spices may be varied as desired. I use cinnamon, cardamom, ginger, cloves and allspice. Try these and others which you may discover on your own. The tea drinking habit in East Africa is the result of British influence, and the spices were introduced to the region by early Portuguese, East Asian and Arab traders.

Drinking tea before a meal curbs your appetite, though it is also often used right after a meal.

"If you know the beginning, the end will not trouble you."

Matunda Ya Tangausi
Ginger Drink

1 can orange concentrate (12ounces)
2 tablespoons ginger, grated
2 cups water
1 fresh lemon or lime
2 tablespoons sugar

1.   Make orange juice following directions on the can.
2.   In a blender, blend grated ginger, squeezed lemon/lime, water and sugar.
3.   Using a large sieve, strain mixture and add to orange juice.
4.   You may add more sugar if desired.
5.   Let stand in refrigerator for at least 1/2 hour before serving to let the ginger flavor blend into the juice.
6.   Serve with any meal or snack.

Serves ten or more.

This recipe was shared with me by a friend from West Africa where the ginger is first boiled and then brewed overnight before it is used in the drink. This process takes out some of the fresh natural herbal qualities of the root. For that reason I prefer to use fresh ginger.

This is an exotic, delicious drink when properly prepared.

"Eat a little, save a little, don't forget tomorrow."

Top: Left-right: Jennifer Froistad, Jody DeChaine, Grace Kuto, Edith *Ratcliffe, Rachel Luswetti at 2000 Chwele Health Clinic officialopening.*

Bottom: Left-right:World Affairs Council of Oregon Women Forum group atclinic official opening-2000

The Hungry Child of Africa

The African child knows all about pain and hunger,
The misery of starving is for the weak and the younger.
Flies crawl around eyes that are tear-filled and sore,
And the world spins by without doing anything more.

The mother who cradles her crying child,
Looks down on her infant, dazed and tired.
With a broken heart she knows her child's fate,
If only she could stop the rivers of hate.

In a world of abundance, a harvest of gifts,
Her child is dying, his head he can't lift.
Hopeless and helpless she stands silently by,
While her heart's blood takes his last breath and last sigh.

Top: Youth at Chwele getting ready for clinic official opening
— 2000

Bootom: Namwela Secondary School students doing a
cultural dance for American visitors — 2006

East African Diet History

In the many works on African cooking, little has been said about the healthy, organic and nutritional values of the traditional African diet. The pre-colonial diet was based on milk, legumes, fruits, vegetables and grains. Among most tribes in East Africa (except for nomads) meat is consumed less frequently in comparison to the western world. (In coastal and lake areas, fishing rather than hunting provides the animal protein.)

Due to their mobile lifestyle, the nomadic tribes in East Africa consume a great amount of meat — which has a high cholesterol content — yet they show the least levels of cholesterol in their blood. Commonly mentioned in early European accounts, the African diet in general consisted solely of sesame seeds *(sim sim)*, rice, corn, millet, beans, peas, squash, pumpkins, yams, sweet potatoes, okra, nuts, collard greens, mushrooms, berries, mangoes, etc., which made for an ideal diet. The production of food in East Africa is mainly hampered by drought, floods and conflict.

In the case of the meat-eating nomads, it was proven that the frequency and length of time spent on physical activity is more important than the amount of fat one consumes. One study by cardiologist M. John Murray of the University of Minnesota, examined the specific components of the Masai diet. The study revealed that 70 percent of the Masai diet consists of animal fat (milk, blood and meat) yet their active lifestyle was the contributing factor to their robust health.

In traditional African cooking salt or sugar are rarely added in the process. Salt and sugar were introduced in the African diet by early travelers and explorers from Arabia, East Asia, Portugal and several European countries — Britain, Germany and France. Other spices appeared in the late 19th and early 20th centuries and were incorporated into dishes.

What is perceived as African cooking today, especially in urban and suburban areas, has been influenced by Arabian, Indian and European flavors and ingredients. During the pre-colonial period, studies showed that hypertension, high blood pressure — a condition associated with excessive salt intake leading to heart attacks and strokes — was almost non-existent among native Africans.

Diabetes was just as rare in pre-colonial times. With the adoption of the western diet and habits, including smoking and the excessive use of alcoholic beverages, diet-related diseases are more common and are more prevalent in urban and suburban areas.

According to studies presented at the Fourth International Conference on Hypertension in Blacks (ICHB) in Nairobi, Kenya in 1989, the rate of hypertension is eight times greater in Nairobi than in the rural parts of Kenya. One particular study conducted by Kenyan medical experts disclosed that the incidence of hypertension among the Masai and Samburu tribes is almost non-existent. Those ethnic groups which have maintained their traditional lifestyles and diets have managed to escape the dilemma of serious health problems.

During the conference it came to light that hypertension has reached epidemic levels among black people all over the world. In the United States black hypertensives suffer two to three times the rate of strokes, twice the rate of heart failure and up to eighteen times the rate of kidney disease as white hypertensives. Based on these trends, some medical experts conclude that black people may have a hereditary trait that is more sensitive to sodium, smoking and excessive alcohol intake. Black people may need to choose their foods more carefully and avoid the harmful elements in their diet and lifestyle.

Top: Namwela Secondary School students, one of the four schools located by the clinic

Bottom: Lewis and Clark students with Chwele Girls' High School students, one of the four schools located by the clinic

Balanced Nutrition

Eating "right" — choosing food for good health — is made easy when we understand simple nutritional facts.

Nutrition is the science of body nourishment and deals with food nutrients, their characteristics, sources and functions. This science reveals the facts of what happens when inadequate, adequate or excessive amounts of nutrients are consumed by the body and discusses the interaction of nutrients in the body.

There are six classes of nutrients the body requires in order to maintain balance and health:
1. Carbohydrates.
2. Protein.
3. Fat.

4. Vitamins.
5. Minerals.
6. Water.

These nutrients are discussed individually here as they relate to the East African diet. Each nutrient has its own particular function yet several nutrients must combine in order to best benefit the body. A balanced diet is achieved by consuming a wide variety of foods on a regular basis containing different nutrients and chemicals.

I encourage you to try out as many recipes as possible. If you are not familiar with the type of food in this book, you are in for a treat of experiencing new and exciting tastes which you can add to your established diet.

1. Carbohydrates

Starches (complex) and sugars (simple) are two main carbohydrates. Complex carbohydrates are the preferred form of carbohydrates for the human diet. The primary function of carbohydrates is to provide energy, which helps the body to maintain temperature and the use of other nutrients.

The major sources of carbohydrates in the East African diet are maize (corn), millet, sorghum, rice, cassava, native sweet potatoes, yams, green and ripe bananas and Irish potatoes. Complex carbohydrates are more popular than simple carbohydrates because most Africans eat the traditional foods and are vigilant about processed foods.

The recipes demonstrate that most foods are eaten in their most original form.

2. Protein

Protein is needed for growth and cell repair — it maintains and builds tissue. People under the age of 18 need more protein than middle aged people. Protein also provides amino acids for the synthesis of all enzymes, all antibodies and certain hormones. Protein serves as a secondary source for energy. If a diet doesn't consist of adequate carbohydrates, proteins are broken down to provide energy, preventing them from performing their primary function. Protein is derived from animal and plant foods.

A typical East African diet is comprised of more plant than animal protein. Plant foods are not only more readily available but are more economical and are healthier for consumption than animal protein. Since the protein in plant foods in incomplete, grains must be served with vegetables in order to provide complementary amino acids.

The most common plant protein sources are: beans, lentils, peas, *ndengu* (mung beans), groundnuts (peanuts), and *sim sim* (sesame seeds). The main animal protein sources are fresh milk, *maziwa lala* (buttermilk), eggs, fish, poultry, beef and game meats. The Masai and Samburu tribes depend more on animal protein than plant protein due to their nomadic lifestyle in more arid areas.

3. Fats

Fat supplies the body with vital fatty acids which are necessary to maintain a healthy balance. Fat carries fat-soluble vitamins (A, D. E, and K), insulates the body and at the same time cushions vital organs.

There are three classifications or fat:

... Saturated fats from animal sources, as well as coconut, palm and hydrogenated oils. Saturated fats are solid or semi-solid at room temperature.

... Mono-unsaturated fats include olive and peanut oil and avocado fat.

... Poly-unsaturated oils include corn, sunflower and all other vegetable oils.

Cholesterol is mostly found in animal fats.

Most health organizations, including the Food and Drug Administration and the American Heart Association, recommend that the average daily diet not contain more than 30 percent fat. Although fat is needed, excessive fat — especially saturated — tends to raise the cholesterol buildup in the body's arteries which in turn may cause coronary heart disease.

Cholesterol comes in low-density lipoprotein (LDL) and in high-density lipoprotein (HDL). It is the latter which leads to heart disease. High blood pressure as well as high blood cholesterol are the main causes for coronary problems. Smoking is the third enemy to good health.

4. Vitamins

Most authorities on nutrition recommend that a well balanced diet contains the required daily supply of thirteen vitamins the body requires.

However, some people — especially in western cultures — feel that taking a multivitamin daily provides additional dietary benefits. This is more necessary than ever because even with organic foods we do not get the nutrition we used to from our food.

There are two types of vitamins, fat-soluble and water-soluble. The fat-soluble vitamins are stored in the body (A, D, E, and K). Water-soluble vitamins (C and the B series) are processed by the body but not stored. Since the fat-soluble vitamins are stored in the body, toxicity can occur if excess amounts are consumed.

Vitamin A helps to build body cells, and is best known for enabling us to see in dim light, and for preventing certain eye diseases. In East Africa, vitamin A is found in milk, carrots, sweet potatoes, *sukuma wiki* (collard greens), kales and other local green leafy vegetables. It is easy to obtain enough of this vitamin as it comes in concentrated amounts, e.g. 1/2 cup of sweet potatoes provides you with 150 percent of the "Recommended Dietary Allowance."

Vitamin D helps in building bone tissue and absorbing calcium from the digestive tract. The Kenyan diet derives vitamin D from fish, fortified milk, and other dairy foods. Since Kenya lies on the equator, there is plenty of sunshine all year which helps convert provitamin 7-dehydrocholesterol in the skin into vitamin D.

Vitamin E protects vitamin A and unsaturated fatty acids from destruction by oxidation. The main sources for vitamin E in East Africa are vegetable oils, green leafy plants, whole grains and egg yolk.

Vitamin K acts as a blood clotting agent. The main sources of vitamin K are green leafy vegetables. The body also produces its own supply in the intestines.

Vitamin C forms the substances that literally hold the cells and the body together. It is instrumental in healing wounds and increases resistance to infections. Kenyan diet derives this vitamin from green leafy vegetables and the plentiful supply of tropical fruits (see glossary) provides vitamin C for the Kenyan diet. Several species of wild fruits are disappearing due to the harvesting of forests caused by the demands of a growing population for firewood.

Vitamin B series:

B (niacin) promotes healthy skin and nerves, aids the digestive system and keeps up our energy level. Natural sources of this vitamin in East Africa are beef, fish, poultry and ground nuts (peanuts). Large doses of niacin lower levels of LDL cholesterol and triglyceride while raising levels of HDL cholesterol.

B$_1$ (thiamin) contributes to the functioning of the nervous system, enhances normal appetite and assists in supplying energy to the body. This nutrient is needed in small amounts. In East Africa it is found in ground nuts (peanuts) and cashew nuts.

B₂ (riboflavin) promotes healthy skin and eyes, and also helps in the utilization of energy. Fresh fruits and *maziwa lala* (buttermilk, sour milk) are excellent sources of this nutrient in Kenya.

B₆ assists in the regeneration of red blood cells and regulates the use of protein, fat and carbohydrates. This vitamin is mainly found in bananas, millet and meats in the Kenyan diet.

B₁₂ helps to maintain nerve tissue and blood formation. This nutrient is only available in animal foods. It is important for vegetarians to take vitamin B_{12} supplements. In Kenya, B_{12} is found in beef, fish, poultry, eggs and other dairy products.

5. Minerals

Minerals are necessary for body building and regulatory functions. Six primary minerals are recommended for daily requirements and include calcium, iron, phosphorus, iodine, magnesium and zinc. Smaller amounts of nine other minerals make up the daily requirement. For the sake of brevity, only calcium and iron are discussed in detail.

Calcium is responsible for maintaining healthy bones and regulatory functions in the blood serum. The best source of calcium is milk — in East Africa fresh milk is mainly served to children. In several tribes, some adults prefer it to buttermilk. Milk is one of the main foods in the high protein diet of the Masai people. Other sources of calcium in East Africa are varieties of wild green leafy vegetables, *sukuma wiki* (collard greens), kale, etc.

Iron combines with protein to form hemoglobin (red substance in the red blood cell) and transports oxygen to all parts of the body. Menstruating and pregnant women require larger amounts of iron in their diet during those periods. (Due to the lack of iron in their diet many expecting mothers are anemic in East Africa.)

Sources of iron include animal liver and other meats which are consumed less frequently. Although legumes are a steady diet, they don't contain large quantities of iron. The type of iron found in vegetable foods is not as easily absorbed in the body in comparison to the iron originating from animal foods.

6. Water

Next to air, water is the most necessary substance for life support. Most people do not think of water as a nutrient, yet it is one of the most important ones. We can go without food for months, but without water, we can only survive a few days. Water accounts for about 60 to 70 percent of our body weight.

Water is a major component of our body tissue and acts as a solvent, regulates body temperature, carries nutrients and oxygen to the cells and washes wastes and toxigens out of our bodies by way of perspiration, tears and urination. Low water intake has been linked to an increased risk of kidney stones in people.

Eight to ten eight ounce glasses are considered the ideal amount of daily water consumption — elderly people, breast-feeding mothers and athletes need more water than the prescribed eight glasses. Ideally, this quantity is in addition to other beverages and is not a substitute. Water is the most ideal thirst quencher since it has neither calories nor harmful chemicals.

Limit the intake of other beverages because some of their contents are not necessarily healthy. Alcohol is a toxic substance; coffee stimulates adrenal glands, while some processed fruit juices contain a lot of sugar and stimulate the pancreas. Soda pop contains sodium and raises body acid. A 12-ounce soda has an equivalent to eight teaspoons of sugar. These drinks tax the body more than cleanse it.

Due to East Africa's tropical climate people drink more water to quench their thirst than any other liquids. (Commercial beverages are expensive.) Drinking the daily required amount of water calls for discipline. For those struggling with that issue, here are some tips to make it easier for you:

1. Use a large plastic container with lid and straw (at least 32 fruit ounces). Fill it with water every morning and let it be your companion for the day. Sip on it frequently, refill it. You may flavor your water with fresh lemon juice or even milk.

2. Just before you go to bed, drink a medium-large glass of water every night. If you drink 64 fluid ounces during the day and 12 fluid ounces at bedtime, you will have supplied your body with the right amount of water.

Remember the human body responds according to Pavlov's theory. Start conditioning your body by drinking more water and your body will soon demand it. Try it. You will be amazed how quickly your habits change.

However, the dilemma is that the U.N. states that at least 80 percent of deseases in Africa are water born

Fiber, though not necessarily a nutrient, is an important part of our diet. Also known as roughage, it is the (rough) material found mostly in many whole foods. Cellulose, a component of dietary fiber helps with digestion and elimination. Some research evidence suggests that the adequate consumption of fiber plays a role in the prevention of some types of gastro-intestinal cancers.

The traditional East African diet is especially rich in dietary fiber which is found in fruits, vegetables and whole grains. Most of these foods are eaten frequently and in their natural form. My favorite comment about the African diet is that we eat our foods the way they were created.

Legumes are of important nutritional value to the African diet. Legumes are comprised of beans, peas and lentils, and are the main source of protein in the diet of most African rural communities. These beans are low in fat, inexpensive and can be prepared in many different ways. Some of your favorite recipes in this book may turn out to be the legume dishes. Beans come in all shapes and sizes and are readily available. The most common varieties in East Africa are kidney beans, black beans, mung beans *(ndengu)*, navy beans, cow peas (black-eyed peas), pinto and red beans.

For years in the western world, beans had the reputation of being the "poor man's meat." However, with recent discoveries on the bean's nutritional value, their reputation is slowly improving, and a good selection of recipes for bean dishes is available. I hope that you try the bean recipes in this book and begin including them in your diet.

All beans except soybeans do not consist of whole protein which can be easily overcome by serving them with rice or other grains, nuts or a small amount of chicken or lean beef which help to flavor the beans. These meat additions complete the amount of protein in legumes by providing complementary amino acids. Beans are also a good source of iron. A cup of most (cooked) legumes supplies about 25 percent of the RDA of iron for women and 40 percent for men. The iron found in legumes however is non-hemo iron which the body doesn't absorb as well as the hemo iron found in animal foods. By consuming foods rich in vitamin C, you can increase the absorption of the non-hemo iron.

Legumes are an excellent provider of fiber in the African diet. They contain about nine grams of fiber per cup

— both soluble and insoluble. Soluble fiber helps lower cholesterol levels and controls blood sugar. The insoluble fiber increases stool bulk, minimizes occurrences of some digestive disorders and may help prevent colon cancer. Black, navy and kidney beans are among the highest in fiber and provide the body with calcium. They are not only a good nutritional choice but are economical, keep well, are easy to cook, and have no waste. It's a good idea to keep a variety of beans in your pantry.

It is true that some people are affected by the gas caused by the sugars in the beans. However, not everyone is a victim of this sometimes exaggerated problem. To prevent gas:

1. After soaking the beans discard the water and boil them in fresh water.

2. Beans should not be served with other gas-producing foods such as cabbage.

3. Consume beans earlier in the day rather than at dinner time.

Groundnuts (peanuts) are the most familiar nuts to Americans but they are not a true nut. According to *The Wellness Encyclopedia of Food and Nutrition,* they are classified as legumes. The name groundnut comes from the way peanuts grow — the peanut pods develop below the ground. The shell and kernel are quite soft before they are dried. The most cultivated peanut in Kenya is the Valencia. It is a sweet red peanut with less oil than the Spanish peanut. (It is not called Valencia in East Africa.)

Groundnuts are important in the African diet because they have more protein than any other nut and their fat content falls in the moderate range. When peanuts are boiled, their fat content is even lower than the oil-roasted ones according to the American Heart Association. Peanuts are a good source of thiamin, niacin and folacin, provide a significant amount of iron and magnesium and are rich in dietary fiber. Valencia dry-roasted peanuts are almost fat free.

My favorite bean recipe, *githeri,* is made with peanuts. You will find it in the "Beans" section of the recipes.

In the United States peanuts are mostly eaten dried and oil-roasted as a snack, in candies or made into peanut butter, all of which contain fat. In Africa peanuts are eaten like other legumes. They are part of a main dish in boiled form pressed for oil or ground into a high-protein flour. We make our peanut paste (peanutbutter) to use in peanut sauces. Delicious! All my recipes use natural peanutbutter which have no additives.

When peanuts and beans make up a portion of the meal, they provide the complete protein which has all nine amino acids.

Voices of Volunteers

I was expected to be living in basic rural conditions and see the effects of poverty when I arrived in Grace's village. But what astonished me was the children's hunger for learning I noticed when I visited with Grace and Paul's extended family in their home. The children were thrilled to have visitors and it was perhaps even more exciting to meet relatives from America.

The opportunity to go to school is a privilege many parents cannot afford. In spite of it, the children are eager for intellectual challenges. Grace's daughters were restless and asked me for notebook paper. They proceeded to make a deck of cards out of these bare sheets of paper and created a *Scrabble* game, including a paper board with triple word scores and those little racks on which to hold the paper letters. The children and young adults were then taught to play their first card game. What was the first card game you learned? *Go Fish* of course!

With *Scrabble* in operation curious people gathered around the table. I wish you could have seen the lights in those kids' eyes; these children were so eager to exercise their minds. Things like paper, pens, a book or a game are rarely available in their village. It was great to watch youngsters who weren't glutted with hyper-stimulating high tech gadgets who used their creativity, as they linked words to other words with this homemade game.

Here in our highly specialized medical world most nurses, while having a broad educational foundation, often end up focusing on one medical field or nursing role at a time. The nurses at Chwele were quite nonchalant and even amused when I asked them if they delivered care to all types of disease and all patients. Of course, they did! Who else? Complicated obstetrics, broken bones, minor surgeries, middle-of-the night emergencies and no nearby doctor to help and a hospital — a thirty-minutes drive — and who can supply the car or bicycle?

These nurses would be heroes in my world, providing care for families with minimal resources, poor transportation and no internet contacts. The women were so excited and grateful for the raincoats and umbrellas I brought as gifts – to keep them dry on their walks to the clinic.
We truly have angels in our midst.

Gail Winterman, RN, MS, CCM
Nurse Case Manager, Eugene, Oregon

My name is Thomas Lwebuga. I am a board member of the *Harambee* Centre. I first met Grace Kuto in 1999 through my wife Kendra who knew her and had fallen in love with the work Grace was doing. My first encounter with her was when Kendra invited me to join her helping Grace in preparing a meal for a fundraiser at OMSI. Monies raised at this event would go to complete the work of building a medical clinic in Chwele, Kenya, where Grace grew up. I agreed to help in the kitchen. It turned out I was the only guy among all these women who were full of excitement, energy and the deep seated belief in the work they were doing.

When I showed up, I was promptly assigned to chop loads of onions. I did my job with big tears running down my face while the women talked and laughed as they prepared the various dishes. At the fundraiser, Kendra and I listened to Grace's talk. I was moved by her story, her shining love for humanity and her pride in her African heritage. Subsequently, the *Harambee* Centre was founded and I continued to attend their events as well as volunteer my time.

In 2002, Grace approached me to serve on the board of the *Harambee* Centre. Having been inspired by the work at Chwele, I accepted and have been part of building the *Harambee* Centre into a sustainable organization connecting people here in the Pacific Northwest to the peoples and cultures of African countries.

Two years later, inspired by Grace, I started helping St. Andrews Matale Senior Secondary School in Rakai, Uganda, my ancestral community. Grace has helped to put smiles on faces of the more than 400 students at Matale, many of them orphaned by AIDS. Through the *Harambee* Centre we have helped the school rebuild their classrooms and set up a computer lab. Now, we are in the process of building a science laboratory (Physics, Chemistry, Biology, and Home Economics) from scratch with the help of ZoomUganda -- www.ZoomUganda.org a project that would not have existed without Grace's initial vision.

In 2007, the *Harambee* Centre expanded the Sister School concept to West Linn High school. This resulted in a powerful cultural exchange between the Kenyan and the West Linn community. Through Grace's initial vision, leaders are being brought along who will serve our world in years to come. She is a social innovator, inspirational leader — a wonderful human being whose grace touches everyone around her. I am privileged to know Grace and to be associated with her work.

Thomas Lwebuga, Nike, Portland, Oregon

Kenya — just the name alone brings to mind so many wonderful people, places and the experiences from my first trip to Africa in 2000. I had learned about many of the places in college in a course I took on the culture of Africa: Nairobi, Mombassa, Mt. Kenya, the Great Rift Valley, Lake Victoria, and the Masai Mara. Being able to visit these landmarks from my studies was a dream come true. But the greatest impact on me as an educator was our group's interaction with the people of Kenya.

Grace and Paul Kuto's families opened their homes and their hearts to our group. Being welcomed into their home by Elizabeth and Job Bwayo was one of my special memories of the trip. Their gracious demeanor made me feel that I had a home in a country that was foreign to me. Rose and Justus Mudavadi also surrounded us with kindness and caring. More family members in Teremi and Chwele were so considerate and thoughtful in making sure that our group was housed, fed and comfortable.

The highlight of this trip was helping with the dedication of the Chwele Health Clinic. We worked hard to prepare the clinic for the celebration by hanging curtains, building flowerbeds and tidying up the grounds around the building. To be part of the dedication was special for me, as contributions from Oregon City High School's International Seminars Program helped Grace (in a small way) realize her dreams in providing better health care for her village.

This trip affected me in a variety of ways. First, it opened the door for two more wonderful journeys to Africa: South Africa-Swaziland in 2001 and Ghana in 2003. Both trips were group Fulbright opportunities with the goal of educating students about the countries we visited. Second, it allowed me to share first-hand experiences with my students, letting them see Africa through a different lens than what mainstream media offers. Finally, it provided me with a new circle of friends whose lives I often share with my students. I believe I have a mission to teach about Africa. I make sure my students always remember, "Africa is Not a Country" but is a diverse and beautiful continent populated with families having needs just like ours: affordable and available healthcare, accessible public education, job security, adequate housing and a nutritious diet. I know that I can help the people of Africa by educating our students in realizing the similarities of our different worlds.

Karmin Tomlinson, Lake Oswego, Oregon
Oregon City High School
I teach International Relations, AP Comparative Government and Politics, and am the International Seminars Director for our Talented and Gifted International Seminars Program/

Our first contact with Chwele was through Grace's delicious cooking, providing meals for many people, who in turn helped to support the building of Chwele Clinic. In 1998 Grace and Paul Kuto invited us to meet their families at Chenjeni and Chwele. This contact with Kenya has led to the founding of Friends University at Kaimosi, in Western Province, a few hours south of Chwele. The clinic has become our touchstone with Kenyan Quakers, which in turn has led us to annual trips since 2005, and into the future as God leads. To my surprise, this contact has brought us a life-changing experience. To know Grace and Paul is to be inspired to follow their example.

Dennis Hagen, Ph.D,

George Fox University Professor Emeritus,

Campus Developer for Friends University at Kaimosi, Kenya

The first time I went to Chwele with my parents, Grace and Paul Kuto, I was six years old. I returned three more times during my middle school, high school and college years. My third visit to Kenya, at age sixteen, had the most impact on me. It was the first time I was truly excited about playing a part of being fully involved in the various projects that were being implemented. I learned so much from working with the clinic staff, organizing supplies and by meeting the patients. I felt empowered to share my gift and love for music by starting a music education cross-cultural experience for children in the Chwele village through their schools with my keyboard and violin. I will always remember the community spirit of unity, interdependence and a continued sense of hope despite hardships. I look forward to continue to serve, as well as witness the growth that continues to enhance this community's quality of life through improved healthcare education programs and eventually, effective micro-credit projects.

Lutomia Kuto, Portland, Oregon

Dear Friends,

My three-week visit to Portland, Oregon, USA, has come to a close. I fly back to Kenya on the morning of Tuesday 23rd, November 1999.

Through my host, The World Affairs Council of Oregon: Women's Forum, I was able to meet with you, share with you and learn many important lessons, in particular diversity in a one-world global village.

I was able to give informative presentations about the Chwele Health Clinic in Kenya, which is supported by the Oregon community. My visit to the schools focused on school cultural exchange opportunities.

I want to thank each and every one of you for making my visit such a fruitful experience. Your profound respect for productive work, equality and tolerance as well as your concern for the plight of the poor encourage me.

You will be glad to know that your effort will facilitate sustainable community-based primary healthcare and education for improved nutrition, access to immunization for infants and the prevention and control of malaria, HIV/AIDS, typhoid fever, cholera, tetanus, polio, diarrhea and other ailments for hundreds of thousands of poor peasant families.

It takes a village to raise a child, is an African proverb that characterizes the spirit of commitment as exemplified by Paul and Grace Kuto who continue to be the catalysts for our two communities — Chwele and Oregon — in realizing a common goal. Let us embrace this spirit of selflessness to nurture our desire to make this world a better place for all people.

Our next assignment on the Chwele Health Project is to be able to install solar power for the refrigeration of essential drugs, water, appropriate sanitation, trunks for storage, transport for mobile health education and computer for data and information management — including feedback to Oregon about happenings in Chwele Village and Clinic.

Once again, thank you!! And be blessed.

Alice Barasa Nabwera

Regional Community Leader, Bungoma, Kenya

My late husband, Prof. Job Bwayo and I were first introduced to the Chwele Health Clinic project in 1995 when my youngest sister, Grace Kuto, who lived in Portland, Oregon, USA, wrote *Harambee! African Family Circle Cookbook*. At that time the clinic was just a small four-wall room which served a student population of about 2,600 and local community of some 15,000 people. She informed us that portions of the proceeds from her cookbook would be used to build a new clinic. No time was lost and she started programs in America to raise funds for the initial construction of the clinic.

My husband and I were excited about Grace's endeavor and became interested in participating in the project. My husband, who was a researcher in HIV/AIDS, had wanted to find a way of reaching this community to educate them on the dangers of this disease and how to help those who were already affected by it. For him, a way was being opened about what he had been dreaming. It was exciting to think that this community would have a better healthcare system.

Since my sister and her husband, Paul, lived several thousands of miles away, they needed someone to oversee the proposed project. We volunteered to be that link between them and the project which was to be constructed in the western part of Kenya, about 350 miles from Nairobi. We were both totally committed to what we volunteered to do because we realized what an undertaking this was going to be.

The first thing we did was to hire a contractor to build the clinic. We settled on a company called Timsales which was ready to do the work. We became the communication link between the builder and the Kutos. Once the contractor and the Kutos agreed on the way to handle the construction, we connected the company to the people at Chwele as this builder was based in Nairobi and had no knowledge of the conditions at Chwele.

In 1998, my husband and I took time off to accompany the Kutos and some volunteers from the United States to Western Kenya for the ground-breaking at the clinic. In the year 2000, we participated in the fundraising for the clinic. Between 1998 and 2006, we have hosted several American volunteers in our homes in Magiwa and Karen while on their way to or from Chwele to work on the project. Apart from hosting the volunteers, during the construction of the new clinic, we had to take time off from our regular jobs frequently to travel to Chwele and check on the progress of the work at every stage and report back to the Kutos in America who in turn had to report to the people who had supported them financially. On completion of the building, we were entrusted with the job of paying the contractor on behalf of the Kuto family, making sure that the work was completed satisfactorily before the final payment was made.

By the time my husband passed away, part of his dream had been realized with the building of this clinic.

Therefore, I am taking on the challenge to complete what we had both dreamed of together. God willing, I hope to start a foundation in his memory to empower HIV/AIDS orphans, widows and grandmothers.

Elizabeth Bwayo, Sister to Grace Kuto, Nairobi, Kenya

My Kenyan safari in 2000 was not in search of wild animals – lions, rhinos, zebras, elephants, wildebeest, Dik-dik – though we certainly saw them, most memorably in the Masai Mara. Safari is the Swahili word for "journey." Collectively and individually, our group of six women from the World Affairs Council Women's Forum were on a journey. Our mission was to make ready and dedicate the health clinic in the Chwele that our inspiring friend Grace Kuto had taken from dream to reality through her enthusiastic and tireless *"Harambee"* (fundraising) efforts in Oregon.

I will never forget the excitement of seeing the solid but bare clinic building in the heart of this small village in Northwestern Kenya. The six of us couldn't wait to start fixing it up for the dedication. Under a hot sun, some of us planted flower beds and engaged curious children in helping us, while others moved old furnishings and medical supplies from the tiny, tin-roofed hut that had previously served the village as a dispensary. The melding of traditions was dramatized by the sight of groups of boys, some decoratively painted with mud, running along the road in preparation for initiation rites, and the spare but crowded Quaker church, where a long service preceded speeches, music and dance performances outside the clinic building. I hold dear the memory of Lutomia Kuto playing "Avé Maria" on her violin during the church service. Almost no one in Chwele had ever seen a violin, as exotic to their ears and eyes as a Dik-dik to ours!

The events in Chwele epitomized the spirit of our journey, which was to connect with the Kenyan people, by observing and showing support for self-help and educational projects. We visited more than a dozen programs, ranging from a computer training center for homeless youth, to village schools, to a women's spinning and weaving cooperative, to a water reserve in the hills outside Nairobi and a meeting with national leaders of Girl Guides, the last arranged by Grace's sister Rose Mudavadi.

I love Grace's family! Among other memories I cherish most is the home-stay with her sister Elizabeth and her husband Dr. Job Bwayo, a towering but quiet man who was then the leading HIV/AIDs researcher in Africa (heart-breakingly, he was killed in a car hijacking in Nairobi in 2007); her sister Rose, whom I had visited in South Africa when her husband Justus was ambassador there; Paul Kuto's brother and cousins, who hosted us in their village compound, not far from Chwele.

My personal safari, my journey, was to imagine what I might have experienced had I pursued the graduate degree in anthropology which I had begun 40 years earlier. But then I was focused on the differences among societies. Now I was more interested in cultural transitions and intersections, in how much we share, how much we can learn from those whose lives are shaped by vastly different circumstances.

Modern Kenya was enlightening. We witnessed passionate activists working for better government and environmental causes. Women are visible in economic and political endeavors. Children who have the opportunity for school, even in the most deprived settings, are eager and dedicated. While many old tribal animosities persist and fester, there is increasing acceptance of diversity and personal readiness to embrace new methods and ways of doing things. Yet the pace of life in Kenya is set by the work of one's hands, the yield of the season, the speed of travel along dirt or pitted asphalt roads, and the setting of the sun. We had no choice but to slow down. And we did. And I miss the sensation, as well as the arrestingly beautiful land and the hospitable people that recall it so vividly to mind.

Joella Werlin, Portland, Oregon

My trip to the Chwele village in Kenya in 2006 has definitely been one of my life's most enriching experiences. As a nurse, it provided me an opportunity to volunteer some of my professional skills and knowledge. Most importantly, I dreamt of such a trip for many years, a trip connecting me to my roots and motherland. Thank you for helping my dream become a reality.

I will never forget my introduction to the life of the villagers, as we bumped over 300 miles of some rough roads from Nairobi to Chwele. Kenya is very beautiful. The land is rich with maize and sugar cane fields, avocado and banana trees. Although the roads and infrastructure from Nairobi to Chwele were neglected and in utter disrepair, there was no reflection of this in the faces of the villagers. They commuted mostly by walking, carrying wares and water pots on their heads. They walked to and fro with astounding pride, striving to survive, day by day.

We were welcomed at the Kuto family compound with warm hugs and greetings. Throughout our entire stay in the village they spared nothing to ensure that all our needs were met. Although these people are very poor, some living in thatched roof dwellings, without electricity, refrigeration, or any modern day conveniences, we were cared for as if we were royalty. We ate three wonderful, healthy meals each day, cooked on a stove simply made from three large stones. Without running water, the young ladies assured hand hygiene by pouring water over our hands at each meal, serving with warmth and beautiful smiles. They shared many family recipes and family traditions as we sat around the table and ate together.

The nurses at the Friends Chwele Mission Dispensary portrayed the same spirit of warmth, pride and generosity as the others in the village. This clinic serves an area of over 57,500 people. Many of these people would not have access to medical care, due to lack of finances, resources, or transportation. This dispensary has been the difference between life and death for hundreds of people since it opened.

This dispensary/clinic was operated by two certified nurses, two nurse techs and a lab technician. It was absolutely astounding watching these women work. They were completely committed to saving the lives of the villagers and treat 10-50 people per day, with such ailments as malaria, typhoid, dehydration, diarrhea and upper respiratory infections. They also treat injuries sustained in accidents and domestic abuse. This clinic is committed to community health and preventative care. They drastically reduced the number of malaria cases by distributing mosquito nets to many of the villagers who could not afford them. Prenatal care, immunizations and family planning services are provided at a low cost. These nurses go the schools, churches, and other public forums to distribute information about HIV/AIDS prevention. They provide important life sustaining and medical care to the victims of HIV/AIDS

The clinic staff provides these services, often without a pay check (sometimes there is not enough money for payroll). They survive by eating the vegetables grown in their gardens and by borrowing from one another. The charge nurse stated, "We are Christians. We are nurses. We have a call. We work not for pay, but to take care of our patients."

My last day at the Chwele Missions Dispensary was precious and memorable. One of the young village women arrived at the clinic in active labor. This young mother-to-be took the pain of labor without making a sound and delivered a six-pound baby boy. One of the nurses commented, " We Kenyan women are strong; we don't cry at childbirth."

The new mother had no soft blankets, diapers or baby clothing, used her scarf to wrap her baby, who was welcomed joyfully into the world as a Kenyan.

I returned to the Kuto compound that evening, full of emotions and tears, having been present at the birth of this baby boy. The house was full with women attending a village meeting. They broke out in song when I entered the house and I broke out in tears which disturbed the women. When I explained that I was crying tears of joy, they all cried with me, danced and sang around me in celebration of the birth of this child.

Grace, I will forever thank you for this opportunity. I applaud your dedication to Chwele and surrounding villages. God Bless you always!

Gwen Talkish, RN
Pittsburgh, Pennsylvania

I had the honor in 2000 of leading a delegation of the Woman's Forum of the World Affairs Council of Oregon to dedicate the Chwele Health Clinic in Chwele, Kenya. To be part of Grace Kuto's long life dream of finally providing medical services to the community she grew up in was a memorable occasion for all members of the delegation.

Jackie Goldrick, President and Co-Founder of the *Harambee* Centre, Portland, Oregon

After dreaming for many years of returning to Kenya, I was able to do so in 2004 with my family. I worked with women to enhance the community's understanding in education and health issues.. Contrary to the kids in my mother's village, I have always had an opportunity to go to school. There were hardly any complaints from the children in Chwele about their circumstances. Everyone had an infectious smiles for us. This made quite an impression on me because I remembered how eager the children were to have an education. I worked harder whenever I would think about how much these children hungered for learning.

It was truly a blessing for me to give back to the my Kenyan community. My time in Kenya was among the highlights of my life. I strongly recommend taking the time to go overseas in a volunteer capacity, as it can truly make a difference in people's lives. I came away changed. The women, the children and my family whom I met during this trip undoubtedly inspired me to be part of their community through giving. I am now raising my daughter, Malaika Grace with a sense of cultural heritage and I am teaching her to appreciate the resources she has and to learn to give to her community

Mary Kuto Oliver, Beaverton, Oregon

I Was Embraced

When I first arrived in Kenya, I was amazed to see so many people walking, even when it was dark. I asked "Where are these people going in the middle of the night?" My hosts told me that they were going to their jobs, many of them traveling on foot up to 20 miles a day. Yet they said these folks didn't seem to mind. This amazed me!

During my visit I continued to see local people cheerfully doing things that my fellow Americans would consider too difficult, uncomfortable or tedious. And they did these things without complaining. I was ashamed at the laziness of my own life as I saw people carrying large loads on their heads, with a baby strapped to their backs. Often they would be smiling and singing. The friendliness and openness of the people will forever stay with me. They went out of their way to get to know me and offer friendship. This left a permanent impression on me. I felt no loneliness, stress or discomfort as a visitor.

I came home and was aware of the material wealth of my life, but missed the spiritual wealth of the Kenyan people. They have often lived with much less than most of us and are amazed at the number of shoes or clothes we have, the amount of food we eat or the size of the houses in which we live. Just a small amount of what we have is shared among many and appreciated more than we can imagine.

After being there to open the clinic I was renewed in my commitment to share my abundant life with others who are so beautiful and real. This deepened my life in ways I had yearned to experience.

I will always carry Kenya in my heart and feel at home with its people. Just thinking about it makes me want to start saving for a trip back.

Kathy Price. Tacoma, WA

The Miracle of Solar Power

In June 2001, I was given the blessing of visiting Chwele. I went with Chuck and Nancy Marshall for the purpose of installing a solar electric power system on the Chwele dispensary. At that time, the power lines stopped about ten miles from town. There was no electricity anywhere in town. Chuck was the brains and I was the brawn. We installed the system which powered lights and a refrigerator in the dispensary.

I was impressed with the generosity of the people there. I have never seen poverty at this level, and yet they gave. Janet and her daughter Angela put us up in their house and fed us, the town mayor drove us back and forth in his 1965 Peugeot pickup to the hospital in a neighboring town to where the supplies were shipped. Geoffrey was at my side helping in every way he could. He was waiting for me at the street in the morning, and worked with me all day. To say I'll always remember Chwele is an understatement. My memories of the vilage and its people are still vivid, and will be, until I refresh them with my next visit.

Dale Janzen. McCall, Idaho

The facility and equipment that saved my life:

During and throughout the year 2001, I felt weak, thirsty and was urinating all the time. On December 31 of the same year, I visited Chwele Friends Dispensary which had recently been equipped with almost all hospital facilities by Northwest Medical Teams International in Portland, Oregon, U.S.A.

Through tests using the equipment, it was discovered that I was suffering from diabetes which had brought sugar levels so high that I couldn't simply be healed completely. They recommended that I use insulin injections.

I really lost weight during that time. To continue using insulin at home I needed a refrigerator for storage which I did not have. Because of the equipments supplied to the dispensary I am able to store insulin in their refrigerator. I would have died had it not been for this facility.

For all these years, I have been on insulin stored for me. The difference in my health is quite noticed. I'm now fairly healthy compared to that time. Everybody around me bears the same witness.

George Wekhui (Grace Kuto's brother), Chwele, Kenya

First hand experience at Chwele Health Clinic:

People around the area are impressed with the services that we give and also by the quick services we do to our patients by not leaving them to stand in line for long hours. They get their services and then leave the place when they are satisfied.

Laboratory services offered are up to date (though some are not offered) but patients are happy since other health facilities around don't offer them. The clinic is fully equipped with enough drugs and there is little complaint from patients since they are well served. They are not sent away to purchase their own drugs like other health facilities do. Our patients are well cared for — for example, now malaria cases are kept for observations, T.B. cases are offered free treatment, HIV/AIDS patients get free drugs from the facility. We refer cases such as anemia and surgery. People are very reluctant to go away for referrals due to lack of transport and lengthy service. An ambulance is desperately needed to give more patients better access to our facility. Some die from dehydration due to malaria for lack of transportation to our clinic. Some cases are not handled well because of understaffing of nurses. We, the staff at Chwele Health Clinic again thank our friends in Oregon for building this clinic.

Nurse Willmina, Chwele, Kenya

God was kind enough to remind Grace Kuto of the need to perfect his creation in Chwele through provision of medical care. People, particularly students of this area, were facing exstinction, dying and being helpless due to lack of close and humane medical attention.

I have worked and stayed in this area now for 14 years and have experienced the great transformation the clinic has brought in people's health. It has not only reduced death, but given better health options and hope to residents.

The estimated student population in four schools is about 3,000 with support staff, families, and people who provide services pushing the number of this core community to about 10,000 who entirely rely on this facility for survival and medical attention.

In my school Namwela, we have our students treated and even receive counseling services on voluntary basis. It is a twenty-four-hour service facility that seriously lacks personnel to handle the demand. Even the infrastructure is not enough and cannot handle all cases. I am happy our friends in U.S.A care enough for us and are doing so much. Let them know that they have made a difference in the lives of many people here. This community is determined to join in helping raise funds for the new community centre which will provide programs for small business activities, orphans, grandmothers, widows, dental healthcare etc.

This is a must succeed facility if we are to survive and live. We thank you for your care and you will be blessed in return.

One person, a teacher by name Gertrude Wanjala gets excited when you mention Chwele Clinic. She pauses and after smiling says she owes her life to the clinic. In a period of six years she has given birth three times including birth of twins in the clinic. Every time she was due, she simply walked to the clinic without her husband who is the current Deputy Principal of Namwela Secondary School. He was only called on all the occasions to pick up his wife and the new born. Every birth has been a safe delivery and she parades the healthy kids as a testimony. She is grateful to the clinic and wishes that it expand to serve more people.

Principal Richard Sabwami
Namwela Secondary School
Chwele, Kenya

Harambee with Grace

The Humbling Journey of Chwele Health Clinic

There are so many humbling moments to talk about, but with only so much room in this publication, I can only tell about a few. I am including the historical background which explains who I have become today.

Born by Grace

The humbling moment and the beginning of this story started the day I was born. Grace is my Christian name. My African name is Nasiebanda which means "survivor" because I was overdue at birth. My mother encountered severe health problems at the end of her pregnancy and it was uncertain whether she and I would survive. When we both made it, my mother said to my oldest sister, "Nora, we are both alive only by the grace of God." The two women decided to name me Grace. My name constantly reminds me of God's grace in my life and the blessings I have as a bearer of this name. I love the meaning of my given African name as well because I have survived so many ordeals in life. I am a survivor!

Loss of my Parents

My father died when I was three years old and Mother left us six years later. I was extremely close to my mother, even though my older sister, Nora, had taken me on to raise. My most vivid memories of my mother are the beautiful, melodious African and Christian songs she taught me in expression of her faith in her African heritage and her God respectively. She also told us many Bible stories and African fairy tales every night at bedtime. Lovingly, she would tell the stories until every one of us fell asleep — one by one.

Before she died, I had dropped out of school for three months and sat by her side every day. At that age, I did not realize that she was dying. Intuitively, I felt a compelling urge to protect her from harm. Vigilantly, I watched the village visitors who came to wish her well, pray for her, to see if they would say anything to upset or harm her. I was her ultimate protector. I faithfully chased the flies that frequently visited her bedside to claim the space she occupied. We rarely spoke but sometimes solemnly sang as if time together would never end. Sometimes we would sing until I cried, but Mother would always reassure me with her presence. When she became too sick to be at home, she was admitted to a government hospital in Bungoma, a town about fifteen miles away from Chwele. While she was there, we could not afford to go there by bus. One early morning at five o'clock, I joined some of my brothers, sisters and family friends to walk to the hospital. I remember walking for many hours on end. Every now and then I would ask, *khuola sa ngapi* — are we are getting there? Once in a while, I would l refuse to walk. I was in tears and in protest of my burning feet since we had no shoes. This slowed down the whole group and one of my brothers would carry me on his back for a while. My sister, Elizabeth is a few years older than me and she too was experiencing the same foot burning problem but never complained even once. I don't even remember how many hours it took us to arrive at the hospital but at the end of that day, Elizabeth's and my feet were so swollen we could barely walk. That was the last time we saw mother alive. We never knew what disease took her precious life at age fifty-eight, because during the colonial time, the doctors did not communicate that information to families.

The day we buried our mother was my humbling moment of the tremendous loss I experienced. It seemed like the whole world came to say good-bye to this "Mother Theresa" stature-and-character-like woman. Among the multitudes of people, I got lost from my family. I found myself in the middle of a tightly packed group of people who were absorbing the African rain like sponges. I looked up at the wet sky and the rain was angrily coming down to wash my meek tears off my face. In that most hopeless moment, I suddenly remembered the Bible story of Jacob's twelve sons who were rescued by their youngest brother, Joseph, during the days of famine. I thought to myself, I am the youngest and the 12th child. Some day, God will take me far away from this village so that I can do something good for my brothers and sisters. That was my comforting moment that leaned on my mother's legacy of story-telling. Today, I carry her torch as I tell different stories about my cultural heritage, the plight of Africa, the children of Africa, the pride of Africa and the unheard voice of her people.

The Loss of our Daughter

While we were students at Portland State University, my husband and I decided to have children. We visited Kenya for four weeks while I was five months gestation. Returning home, we went to see my doctor the next day for a regular check-up. He diagnosed me with toxemia of pregnancy and I was admitted to the hospital the same day. After about two months of complete bedrest in the hospital, I was devastated when I had a still-born baby at eight months gestation.

Leaving the hospital without the baby was almost harder than loosing the baby, yet we came away most humbled by God's grace, for I had once again survived. Though we experienced many months of deep grief, we had to continue with our classes at the University because if we hadn't, we would have been deported immediately.

It was His grace and gift of faith that later carried us through our next two severely toxemic pregnancies and survival of our two pound and one and one half pound babies.

The Moment of Revelation

While I was in Kenya in 1994, I took my ten-year old niece, Joy, to the one-room Chwele Health Clinic because she had malaria. The room was divided in two sections by a sheet of cloth. While Joy was being examined on the other side of the sheet, I waited a while. It was raining outside, so we had to keep the wooden windows and door closed. This made the inside of the clinic uncomfortably dark in the early afternoon. My mind started reflecting on how ill I was each time I had the toxemia of pregnancy and how I came so close to dying. I thought of all the women who die in this village due to child-bearing complications and no one ever knows the specific condition that prematurely takes their precious lives. They seem well one moment, and the next moment they are gone forever often taking their unborn child with them.

It is assumed by their loved ones that someone might have poisoned them with the last meal they ate or put a spell of *vudu* on them. In a true moment of revelation, I realized that if I had not left the village, I would not be alive. That hit me like a bomb and I felt such grief for myself. I came out of that clinic with a humbled spirit and a new appreciation of life, mine and of those in the village who had raised me. "I knew God had brought me out." Upon returning to Portland, Oregon, I completed the *Harambee! African Family Circle Cookbook* in 1995 whose partial proceeds were donated to build a new clinic which could offer more and better healthcare services to the community.

Chwele Was Honored

Former Senator Mark O. Hatfield of Portland, Oregon honored the Chwele Health Clinic project by coming on board to speak on its behalf in 1998. I first contacted his office at Portland State University requesting his honored presence. Jane Gravel answered the phone and asked if I had anything in writing about the project for him. I faxed her a copy of my brochure. The next day, I thought how he did not know who I am, or where Chwele is located and of course he would not accept the invitation. I hurriedly called Jane back, and asked her to hold off talking to him because I wanted to send him some testimonial letters from individuals and organizations I had worked with in the Portland community on this project.

Jane replied that he had already agreed to speak at the fundraiser and requested that I meet with Sue Hildick (now Sue Kline). I met with Sue — who was then the OHSU Government Relations Liaison — within days. She listened to my story about the clinic and suggested to the Senator that he met with me before he spoke at the event. We met shortly thereafter. He has the warmest handshake I have ever received from the western hemisphere. I was so humbled and honored to meet him. He told me of how he had initiated a bill in Congress to boycott Uganda's coffee to disarm Idi Amin's tactics that were being funded by the coffee sales. The bill was passed and Kenya was the beneficiary of the aftermath. I immediately came up with a plan that could suit his level of participation. I contacted the World Affairs Council of Oregon Women's Forum of which I was a member and asked for ... help! With the woman power behind it under Wendy Amin's direction, we coordinated an impressive *Harambee!* Which raised more than $15,000 for the clinic construction.

Helpless Moment at the Old Clinic

While we visited the Chwele community with Professor Dennis and his wife, Janet, to join in the groundbreaking of the clinic in 1998, I witnessed a distressing moment for a young teenage student from the Chwele Girls' Secondary School. While we were attending a meeting with the community building committee in front of the old clinic, a number of students who were carrying a young woman came rushing to the clinic. The student was having convulsions. They quickly placed her under the shade of a tree in front of the clinic and one of them rushed in to call for the patient attendant. She came out, looked at the motionless patient and told the students that there was nothing she could do for her, because she did not know what was wrong. I thought to myself, this is the reason we should build a better clinic as soon as possible.

The patient started having convulsions again and the other students started to cry as we watched helplessly. The nurse finally suggested to the students to take the sick girl to her house and everybody assembled will pray for her. The students quickly picked her up and literally ran to the patient assistant's house just a few yards away. Eventually, a car was found to take the girl to Lugulu Hospital where she recovered from what turned out to be cerebral malaria — a highly dangerous form of malaria that attacks the brain tissue.

The Aroma of Stories Fill the Kitchen

Upon return to Oregon, I immediately decided to write *Harambee! African Family Circle Cookbook* so that I could contribute to the cost of the clinic construction. After the book was published in 1995, my cooking for larger numbers of people took on a life of its own. My friends Marianne Slabough of Portland, Jesika Dalizu originally from Kenya and Jossie Kpobe-Tee from Nigeria, enthusiastically helped me with marketing the book while Tigard Community Friends Church did the financial accounting for the project. Linda Swenwold was my angel at TCFC. Pricilla Downing was my angel at Multnomah Presbyterian Church.

I had convinced myself that I could continue to do the cooking for hundreds of people without help. However, without asking several angels usually showed up when I most needed them.

I needed their stories to keep my batteries going as well. Story telling is synonymous with cooking in Africa. My friend, Chip Edie, showed up in our family at the peak of these cooking experiences which bound us together like sisters. She lived with us for almost three years. She was the first American I met who totally understood my way of cooking, thinking, and of writing down my thoughts. She could literally read my mind and organized my path before I would get there. We deeply embraced each other's cultures through cooking and story telling.

Carol Briggs was one of my angels too. I would never tell her when I was planning to cook for hundreds of people because I knew she would try to do too much for me. Somehow, she always found out about my upcoming events, and would show up with a crew consisting of her 21-year-old grandson Derik and his unsuspecting friends. These angels helped to cook African food and transport it to the serving location. One time, she even showed up with her boss. It was during one of these cooking sessions in 2005, when Carol and my sister Elizabeth met for the first time and shared their kitchen stories that bound them together forever.

Another friend, Thomas Lwebuga, originally from Uganda, was always the only man who ever cooked in my kitchen that was filled with story and food aromas spiced with empowered women's energy. He never talked much but later we discovered that he had been quietly crying from chopping dozens of those unforgiving onions, but he was not going to let the women know that this task made him cry.

Once, my friend Marianne Fry, joined us to make *mandazis* (fried bread). She managed to decorate herself thoroughly with the flour as she diligently rolled the dough while I watched the mandazis puff and hug each other in the hot, simmering oil. And, there was Jennifer Froistad, who peeled and crushed zillions of garlic cloves until her fingers complained. All these gracious volunteers and many others made it possible to raise the funds to build the clinic in my village. I am forever grateful to all who ever took part.

Opening of Chwele Health Clinic

Through the World Affairs Council of Oregon, under Jackie Goldrick's leadership, my husband and I with five others (Jennifer Froistad, Jody DeChaine, Karmin Tomlinson, and Joella Werlin) including our daughter, Lutomia went to Chwele to join the community for the official opening of their clinic. I had diligently worked for five years to get to this point. By this time, I had cooked African dinners with help from volunteers for as many as 400 people in a seating in five different States-Alaska, California, Michigan, Oregon, and Washington.

I had done keynote speaking in all these states. Participating in the clinic opening was the highlight for me in this whole journey. On that day, I reflected on so many experiences that had been part of my life thus far. I mostly thought of my mother that day and silently cried tears of grief mixed with joy. I thought how she used to serve her community so lovingly when she was alive. I thought of how my father insisted that his daughters had to go to school just like the boys in the village and how this trickled down to all of us through my older sisters. Multitudes of people attended the opening of the new clinic just like they did a generation ago when my mother had passed on. One of my brothers-in-law,Ambassador Joseph Muliro was very ill and had not been out of bed for at least two weeks prior the opening. Like the rest of my in-laws, he had been close to my parents. He said that when he woke up on the day, he felt a lifting in his healing that he had not felt before. He had promised mother in his heart that he would go to the opening just to honor her services to the community. He told me all this at the event and expressed his feelings of being blessed just by being there. He had come full circle. That was the last time I saw him alive, but I have always remembered his words of encouragement in this work in which he so believed and practiced as a member of parliament for this constituency.

Another humbling moment for me was being able to spend time with Edit h Ratcliffe, a Quaker missionary nurse who had served at Chwele for more than 45 years. She too came full circle when the new clinic opened. Every community member knew her because she had treated each one of us over the years. She was the presiding guest of honor for the occasion and her keynote address came to us in form of a sermon. She talked of how she decided to become a missionary to Africa. She talked of Jesus' love for the poor and how He asked His disciples during the last supper to serve the poor just as He had demonstrated His love for them by washing their feet despite Peter's refusal.

Solar Power Saves Lives

In 2000, I met Marty McCall of Portland, Oregon who saw right through my heart as we carried on our conversation. I was amazed at how she quickly came up with a plan to have an African at her friends' house, Jane and John Emrick. She and the Emricks called their friends together for a serene but spirited gathering which also welcomed Alice Barasa Nabwera from Chwele community to Portland, to share update news of the clinic. I was so humbled and grateful when later the Emricks informed me that they would match the funds raised at the gathering until we raised enough for installing solar power at the clinic. Within three months we had raised $25,000 for a system that powers the whole clinic, its medical equipment and more importantly, the refrigerator which would enable the clinic to safely store life-saving medications.

Within months, my brother, George, was diagnosed with diabetes and without insulin, he would have died. He and many other patients are forever grateful for the gift of solar power. On behalf of the Chwele community, I am so thankful to Marty McCall and the Emricks, their family and friends for reaching out to this far-away community in such a thoughtful way. The clinic was the first building in the village to have solar power. It has also served as a catalyst for this type of power for the village. Now, several homes are using solar power.

Engineer Chuck Marshall and his wife Nancy of West Linn, Oregon together with Dale Janzen of McCall, Idaho, installed the solar power in 2001. A 40 foot container of medical equipment and supplies were also delivered to the clinic from Medical Teams International in Portland.

American Nurses Visit the Clinic

Gail Winterman, a nurse from Eugene, Oregon came with us to clinic in 2004. Before she left for Kenya, she talked to many of her colleagues for donations and asked pharmaceutical companies to contribute medical supplies. She received positive response for her efforts. She arrived at the clinic equipped to work with the staff to exchange professional and cultural experiences. Her visit was suddenly cut short by the illness of her mother but she left a lasting impression with the clinic's staff who still use the supplies she had brought.

In 2006, Gwen Talkish, a nurse from Pittsburgh, Pennsylvania accompanied us to the clinic. She was the first Africa American volunteer to Kenya on our trips. She had always wanted to go there since she was a little girl because she has always considered Africa her home. Like any other American visitor we had brought home, she was welcomed with much warmth. However, her hosts started to speak to her in Swahili or our vernacular, until they realized that she spoke neither of the two languages. Many said that she resembled so many of our ladies in Kenya that they gave her a native name — Nekesa (born during harvest time). She so deeply immersed herself in the professional and social culture of the Chwele community that by the time she left, she was one of us. She was blessed attending the birth of a baby at the clinic on her last day. She had insisted on staying to help with the birth.

When she arrived at our house later that afternoon, the village women were visiting with us to talk about their community activities. As she entered the house, they all broke out in song to welcome her back. Gwen broke out in tears and the women thinking they had upset her, embraced her to comfort her which made her cry even more. When she finally settled down, she explained that she had cried tears of joy, because she just delivered a baby at the clinic. Our guests broke out in song again to congratulate her and sing and celebrate the new baby.

Tragedy Strikes

Our world came to a screeching halt on February 4, 2007 when we received the tragic news that my sister Elizabeth, my brother-in-law, professor Job Bwayo, a world renowned HIV/AIDS vaccine researcher, .our friend, Carol Briggs of Portland, Oregon, and Elizabeth Butane of

Australia had been carjacked and critically shot. My brother-in-law had not survived the shooting.

My husband Paul, my niece Christine McCulloch, and I immediately left for Kenya. We found my sister and Carol still in intensive care units at Nairobi Hospital under the care of Oral Surgeon Eric Kahugu. We buried my brother in-law while these two women were still fighting for their dear lives.

We were then informed by Dr. Kahugu that though Kenya had the expertise to treat these patients, they did not have the equipment to do so. He recommended that we explore other alternatives outside Kenya. I asked him if he has heard of Oregon Health and Sciences University where I work in Oregon. He said he is aware of this medical University's good reputation and I asked him if he knew Dr. Assael. He smiled and said, "Leon is my mentor and I would trust him to provide excellent care for any of my patients." We brought Elizabeth and Carol back to Portland, Oregon with us in March, 2007, accompanied by a nurse, for them to receive care from OHSU.

We are so grateful to our church, Tigard Community Friends Church, who coordinated fundraising for the two women's initial medical expenses. As the time of this writing (May, 2008), they have both received more that ten reconstructive surgeries each and are scheduled for more. Elizabeth plans to return to live in Kenya when full treatment is complete in early 2009.

Our family takes this opportunity to thank each and everyone who in any way played a role in contributing to Elizabeth's and Carol's healing through financial and prayer support. I take this opportunity also to thank my office administration staff and faculty at the OHSU School of Dentistry for their moral support which I could not have survived this ordeal without. I am so blessed to have a dean and manager with very high human values. Elizabeth and Carol have come a long way together and the bond between them is no less than Siamese twin closeness.

After this tragedy, my role in community work simply stopped and I especially thank *Harambee* Centre board members for allowing me space to support my sister's and our family's healing. A few weeks ago, the sun slowly started rising up in my heart. Since I had foregone several years in fundraising for Chwele Community Development, I wanted to use the energy I feel now to fulfill this dream — revise this book to raise funds for the community development. So thank you for joining me in this work by using this book. It makes a great gift too!

About the Author

Grace Kuto, employed at OHSU for over 20 years, the co-founder and Vice President of Harambee Centre, Inc., was raised as an orphan in western Kenya. She embodies the benefits captured in the phrase "It takes a village to raise a child." Grace and her husband Paul, both graduates of Portland State University, live in Portland, Oregon, USA with their daughter, Lutomia. Their older daughter, Muyoka (Mary) and husband, André Oliver have blessed them with a grand daughter, Malaika Grace.

A gifted speaker and educator, Grace has touched the lives of thousands of students and teachers throughout the Pacific Northwest of the United States through her classroom tested "Africa is Not a Country" curriculum and partnership with the K-12 Education Program of the World Affairs Council of Oregon since 1979. She cooks delicious East African meals for a multitude of schools, families, corporate and church communities to support the Chwele Community Development and other local projects. Grace has served on several boards including the World Affairs Council of Oregon, the Multicultural Resource Center and American Friends Service Committee (North Pacific Region). She also co-hosts the Africa Roundtable edition of the Africa On Fire! News Broadcast on KBOO Radio.

Though she has lived in Portland for more than 30 years, she remains devoted to the call of her village in her homeland. She has worked tirelessly to educate, connect and enrich her African and American communities.

Recommended Reading

African Cooking; Laurence van der Post; Time, Life Books, 1970.

The Africa News Cookbook; African Cooking for Western Kitchens; Tami Huttman and African News Services, Inc., Viking Books, 1985.

A West Africa Cookbook; Ellen Gibson Wilson, M. Evens and Company, Inc., 1971.

Cooking the African Way; Constance Nabwire and Bertha Vining; Lerner Publications Company, 1988.

Kwanzaa: An African-American Celebration of Culture and Cooking; Eric V. Capage; William Morrow and Company Inc., 1991.

A Safari of African Cooking; Bill Odarty; Broadside Press, 1971.

Tropical Leaf Vegetables in Human Nutrition; H. A. R. C. Domen and G. H. J. Grubben; Amsterdam and Curacao; Royal Tropical Institute and Orphan Publishing Company, 1977.

Principles of Nutrition; Eva D. Wilson, Katherine H. Fisher, Pilar A. Garcia; John Wiley and Sons, 1979.

The Wellness Encyclopedia of Food and Nutrition; Sheldon Margen, M.D.; Random House, 1992.

The Land and People of Kenya; Michael Maren; Lippincott Junior Books, 1989.

Glossary

Cereals/Breads: cornmeal mash *(ugali)*, cornmeal and millet, porridge, *mandazi, chapatis,* rice.

Meats: Beef, mutton, lamb, chicken, fish, rabbit.

Carbohydrates: Sweet and Irish potatoes, green bananas, plantains, *cassava* (yucca).

Dried Beans and Peas: Red beans, mung beans, cowpeas, pinto beans, kidney beans, black-eyed beans, lentils.

Fruits: Pineapple, papaya *(pawpaw)*, lemon, lime, passion fruit, mango, guava, tomato, berries.

Vegetables: Over 30 varieties of green vegetables are eaten in East Africa alone. The more common ones and those which have known names in English are: collard greens *(sukuma wiki)*, kale, bean leaves, cowpea leaves, pumpkin leaves, cassava leaves, spinach, cabbage, sweet potato leaves, mustard greens, okra.

Dairy Products: Sweet milk, buttermilk *(maziwa lala)*, cheese.

To order additional copies of:

Harambee! Stories and Recipes from the African Family Circle
($20.00 + $3.50 Shipping and Handling)

or contact
Taste of Africa for catering services in the Portland area

Phone: 503-245-3812
E-mail: kutop@comcast.net

Send a donation for the Chwele
Community Development to:
Tigard Community Friends Church
P.O. Box 230117
Portland, OR. 97281